BASICS

A BEGINNER'S GUIDE TO LIGHTING DESIGN

Peter Coleman

ENTERTAINMENT TECHNOLOGY PRESS

Educational Series

BASICS
A BEGINNER'S GUIDE TO LIGHTING DESIGN

Peter Coleman

Entertainment Technology Press

Basics
A Beginner's Guide to Lighting Design

© Peter Coleman

First edition published June 2006 by
Entertainment Technology Press Ltd
The Studio, High Green, Great Shelford, Cambridge CB2 5EG
Internet: www.etnow.com

ISBN 1 904031 41 2

A title within the
Entertainment Technology Press Educational Series
Series editor: John Offord

CODE / BLDS001

CONTENTS

ACKNOWLEDGEMENTS

With thanks to:

Jane Coleman, Pru Coleman, Mike Jarvis and Joanna Jarvis.

My proof readers, who have kept me on the straight and narrow path.

And all at Stage Electrics who have given me encouragement and support.

INTRODUCTION

For anyone not familiar with *Basics – a Beginner's Guide to Stage Lighting, Basics – A Beginner's Guide to Stage Sound* and *Basics – A Beginner's Guide to Special Effects,* I should explain straight away that the aim of this book is to provide – hopefully – a simple explanation of the topic listed.

In the first three *Basics* books I have said that they are *"not intended to be a complete reference work"* and I suppose this one isn't going to differ much. But wait a minute, this is the design element, so perhaps you should expect something a little more concrete, a little more complete.

Quite right too. But perhaps you will allow me just one qualification of the title and you may think a rather obvious one, since I'm the author. "It's *my* guide and interpretation to the design of performance lighting." Yes, I know it sounds rather silly, but you will know that in all walks of life, all people will have their own tried and trusted methods to achieve their goals in work or at play. So, for lighting design, these are *my* methods and thoughts which have worked in a wide variety of performance venues, and I hope you will find even just a small number of them of help to you.

Of course there's no guarantee that what this book contains will fit happily in with your ideas or needs in connection with designing lighting for your event – that's always going to be a risk.

So just what are you likely to get from me, in the area of 'design'? For some, perhaps only an insight into one interpretation of the design process, and I do mean the *design process*. In reality of course, it all means very little if you can't actually put your design ideas into practice and what can stop you from doing this? Well, those two evils of most of our desires – time and money – can, and probably in that order. But don't despair, I'm not about to suggest the employment of massive amounts of equipment and production budgets that run into tens or even hundreds of thousands of pounds.

The really difficult thing about lighting design and the specifics that you are probably expecting from this book, is that it's an all or nothing sort of topic. Across the range of performance requirements and venues, and of course your own individual expectations, it's very hard to give the definitive "How to do it" information. What will be critical for one style and discipline will not be so for the next user in a different venue. However, there are quite a few things that cross all the boundaries of all lighting design and it's these areas that I hope *Basics* can help you with.

I suppose if there's one single issue that will govern and affect your lighting design efforts it's the transition between the concept and the hardware involved. This fact in itself is such a broad issue, open to a wide range of interpretation, that it's almost impossible to provide the correct guide and level of advice to every participant.

There are so many variables in just how you can approach your task of lighting design. For instance, will your design be based upon cost or time? That is the cost of the level of equipment needed to put your ideas in practice and of course the time it will take to do it. These two factors are often linked, so much so that you really can't consider one without the other.

Some would say, perhaps quite rightly, that time and money should not stand in the way of artistic interpretation. Well at some levels I'm sure that is a sound and reasoned view, but perhaps for the majority of us, a more realistic view of life may force us to at least compromise our artistic ideals, if only just a little. And what of your personal expectations? Are you dealing with your own requirements or are you being tasked to deliver someone else's ideas?

Of course the size, scale and location of the event will have some bearing upon your design and, being *Basics,* this book is hardly going to assume your first efforts are to be the lighting of a major production at the Royal Opera House, but as you read on you may think that's what I'm talking about. Hopefully much of the information will help those users at the smaller end of the performance lighting scale.

For those of you familiar with the other *Basics* books, you will know that I am fond of providing alternative titles, but there's not much more to say or explain that's not in the "Lighting Design" part of this title. But there is something, which may put it all into context and ensure that none of us get too serious about it all.

Within the theatre industry there is a lovely story, which I am sure is true. Many years ago, during the rehearsals for a Royal Variety Show, an eminent lighting designer of the day responsible for the lighting of the event asked a not unreasonable question of one of the star performers: "Mr Morecambe, how would you like the lighting?" To which came the now famous reply, "On, yes I think we'll definitely have it on!" Enough said, so "On" it will be.

And finally, as you would expect during the course of writing this book, I have been constantly rereading, correcting and altering things. Much of this has involved editing the layout and I confess I'm still not 100% certain that it's all in the right order. This isn't an excuse or even an apology; it's really my explanation of why it may at first seem rather disjointed. It's very difficult to prioritise just what the most critical points to get across are. Of course, many things will fall into the critical category: firstly your conceptual planning and secondly your ability to deliver this in technical terms, and I confess that writing this from a practitioner's viewpoint has been very difficult. I hope you will forgive those small parts and phrases that may read in a rather condescending way. That wasn't my intention, more a lack of my writing ability. So I hope you can manage to cope with my rambling style, the grand design being that it should all make sense by the final page!

1 THE CONCEPT

Let's get a few ground rules sorted at the outset. Why are you needing information on this topic? Is it your first attempt? Would like to do better but don't know why your last attempt didn't really work? Have you been volunteered for the task? Well, I think this list just about covers what I hope to be able to help you with.

I have to make some assumptions here; well, we have to start somewhere! The lighting I am going to talk about is mainly for theatrical productions normally taking place in a theatre or similar performance space. I have to assume that you will have some understanding of the equipment involved: lanterns, dimmers, control, etc. I covered much of the equipment in *"Basics – A Beginner's Guide to Stage Lighting"*, so we are left to discuss and organise the design and planning of your lighting. For some people the lighting design may be regarded as an irrelevance, something of little consequence: "What is there to design?" they may ask. You simply hang a selection of lanterns up in your venue, drop a few colours in here and there, point them in the general direction of your performers, job done! Why all the hype and discussions about turning on a few lights? Well at least you don't fall into that category of thinking, as it's unlikely you would have picked up this book in the first place.

For those who simply don't know, let me explain that there is a requirement within the performing arts that someone is tasked to organise the lighting. In the early days of electric light, before the days of specific focusing lanterns, I expect the requirement was simply to turn lights on or off. Then came the application of colour; originally the actual lamps were dipped in lacquer, then later coloured glass was used. Remember that in those times the actual light fitting was nothing more than a simple floodlight. Then followed the focusing lantern and the advent of dimming control, if somewhat crudely, using wire-wound resistance dimmers. Eventually, as technology advanced, the lighting equipment evolved into more complex and much better equipment and it was about this time that the role of the *lighting designer* came to be a requirement, partly because the lighting job now needed a degree of understanding and organising and partly because, as with most things, it was cost effective. Someone who knew what they were doing and could obtain good results, saved money and added to the success of the production. Slowly, over the years, and against a grudging acceptance of his skills, the function of the lighting designer shifted somewhat from the original, almost wholly technical job, as it has now grown and holds a place within a production's artistic team.

In today's world the requirement still exists for some just to cover the old concept that somebody needs to look after the technical aspects. In larger, more prestigious events, the artistic ability (or reputation) of the designer is all that matters. At this level the designer is responsible for the ideas and concept of the design and hardly ever gets to touch the actual equipment at all.

What Format is Your Lighting to Be?

So with the brief history lesson over, let's consider how the lighting of your event is to be regarded. For a moment let's not get too bogged down in the nature of the event, as that will come a little later. There are two major conceptual considerations to be made about your lighting:

1) Is it to be a seamless part of the overall event?
2) Is it to be effective in its own right, adding an important facet to the overall end product?

What is it I'm describing here, within these two formats? Well, in the first case, I'm describing what I will class as 'realistic' lighting and in the second 'surrealistic' or 'effect' lighting. How you approach your lighting design will, I suggest, need to be categorised into one of these two formats.

Only two formats? Well remember I am trying to keep this to the *basics,* and I expect many would want to give me an argument about realistic and surrealistic, and within either we need to attempt to portray the many various moods and conditions that apply to the piece we are dealing with. That could be weather conditions, or simply the time of day where the lighting could represent strong shafts of light through a window at midday, or show delicate shades of colour on a backcloth at twilight. Then there's the issue that for lots of so-called realistic lighting, we are trying to mimic an original artificial lighting condition, for example, the inside of a room or building, which in the real world will be lit by an artificial light source such as electric, gas, candles, whatever – the only totally realistic (natural) lighting effect being the natural light, or lack of it, as found in the great outdoors. If you follow this crazy logic, you will end up making the case that everything you produce will therefore be at the surrealistic level. But let's not get carried away here, I think it's an important distinction to make that one form of lighting should attempt to look as realistic as possible, even including the original being lit by artificial light.

A Lighting Coverage

I will start talking about a lighting coverage when working in the realistic format, but this becomes less critical when producing effect lighting. I believe that the lighting coverage is an essential part of realistic lighting, but where you are needing a lighting effect, or indeed lighting for effect, the coverage can sometimes actually get in the way of what you are trying to create.

Within a lighting coverage I will promote the use of multiple lanterns, combining to provide an even and extended coverage of light. I called it seamless and that's exactly how it should look, with no dark holes or hot spots, unless you intend them; but effect lighting follows a different requirement. There is no hard or fast rule about just what constitutes effect lighting, there are no rights or wrongs, it's whatever works for you. This can be a complex arrangement of multiple lanterns from various angles and positions, or it may be just one lantern, lighting your performer or a part of the setting and providing a light source from just one angle.

In the first of many generalisations I will suggest that most productions will probably need or at least benefit from having a lighting coverage, even where the main requirement is for effect lighting. Whereas realistic lighting will rarely benefit from the addition of the effect lighting treatment, the thought process behind this is relatively simple. In a realistic lighting condition, your audience is expecting to see the performers lit in a way that mimics their expectation and imagination of real life; but within effect lighting, realism is not necessarily expected, only the effect. That's all very well, but at some point your audience will probably expect to actually see the performers lit 'normally'. Let's face it, most productions, even those calling for a high degree of effect lighting, probably wouldn't want to sustain the effect content for the total duration of the production. It's at this point that even effect lighting will benefit from some degree of a lighting coverage.

Having got this very important factor of realistic and effect lighting into your thinking, let's carry on with the thought processes involved with your lighting design.

Can You Do It?

If you stop for a moment and just think about it, it's a really tantalising prospect to have an image in your mind of how something that doesn't yet exist will actually look when you put it into place; and here I have some good, or perhaps bad news for you. The bad news is that for some, you may never be able to really achieve the trick. You simply may not have the ability to conceive the image in your mind's eye, at least not in the semi-technical way needed to form the plans required to bring it into reality. The good news is that for the vast majority, you will be able to achieve some level of success. How many people do you know who can't swim or can't ride a bicycle? Well, when we were young we all tried to learn and most of us succeeded to some degree. I find the concepts involved in lighting design a little similar.

One day I might meet with some eminent professor of neurology who can give me the full explanation about the working of the human brain in matters such as these. Maybe the study has already been done, maybe there is an identifiable type of person who has this ability as an automatic function? I rather think that for the majority of us and I'm sure I am one, we *learn* the ability as we might learn a new language.

One thing I hope we can all agree upon, is that to some degree we all have the ability to learn, and having learnt, we have a normal human instinct to mimic, to copy and apply the knowledge learnt into the practical applications of what we do. Extending that ability will bring you to another human trait – original thought – even if only to modify and adapt something experienced and remembered.

So there we are, having labelled some of you as never being able to manage a lighting design process, I've now retrieved the situation by saying that we can all learn and mimic, so that's OK then. Except that, as I recall, there were some things that I tried to learn in my formative years, that I was absolutely useless at (and have been ever since). However, enough of this torture; lets get on with the learning.

Are You an Artist?

In being a designer you are virtually hanging a big sign round your neck that says 'artist', or at least a person who has to deliver an end product allied to some artistic interpretation. But here's the tricky bit, for lots of people who do the lighting design job, it's a fine balance between the technical challenge and the conceptual design exercise, and if that wasn't complex enough, there's the issue of exactly whose design is being used.

If you are asked to design the lighting for a theatrical production, how much of a free hand do you actually have? Are you being asked (probably by the director or producer) to provide *your* interpretation for the lighting, or are you following the ideas and interpretations of others?

It's all very well being told that the next scene to be lit is supposed to be taking place (and thus representative of) a night time exterior, set in a clearing in a forest, but just who decides what shade of overall colour wash should be used? Or just how steely blue the moonlight coverage should look. Or if some of the moonlight should be providing the dappled effect of moonlight coming through the trees and if so, is this effect static or moving? And what is the transition into and out of the main lighting state and what requirements, if any, are there for lighting changes within the scene?

Your way or dealing with this little scenario might include three or more PAR or Fresnel lanterns rigged at one end of your upstage lighting bar (just downstage of the cyclorama) focused predominantly to cover centre and downstage from stage left all the way across to stage right, using a very pale steel blue; while the dappled effect of the light through the trees might use four or more wide angle profile lanterns using small break-up gobos.

These considerations are just a few of the questions to be addressed and of course those tasking you to deliver the lighting will inevitably have their own expectations of it. It may well be that the director and others like your interpretation. On the other hand they may not and suggest that you change it, something that's often very difficult to do quickly.

Is it Your Design?

The other alternative in your design is that it's not your design at all, because you will be following some specific requirements regarding the colour choices, the quantity and even the angle and specific focus of that moonlight and use of gobos to achieve that dappled effect. In short, you aren't really designing anything at all: your role will be to rig, focus and operate. All this of course is dependent upon the team and indeed the individuals you are working with. It's often the case that a team of people working regularly together know and understand the expectations and abilities of each other with very little need for in-depth discussions about it all. Not so when you are brought into a production team and expected to 'perform' you lighting design. So the whole ethos of the design process can, and probably will, change from production to production, location to location.

Teamwork

Whichever method your design is based upon, *your own interpretation or someone else's*, the conceptual starting point for the design will probably need input from a few other people, at least in gathering information about the style of the piece to be lit. The style? Yes, the style, the setting, whatever you call it; your design must work in sympathy with it, alongside which are the parameters and requirements of the venue. You might even describe this as the style of the setting: 'in-the-round', 'concert', 'traditional', 'end-stage', etc. But a different style from the reference to the style of the actual piece to be performed. Let me try to explain myself.

A production of Gilbert and Sullivan, The Gondoliers, might be set in its traditional original time and setting, or be adapted to take place within a modern day setting of Birmingham's canals in the 21st century. You might be performing the piece in a traditional proscenium arch theatre, or on a concert platform with limited technical facilities, as in an outdoor event, or even a theatre-in-the-round venue.

Referring back to my 'realistic' or 'effect' formats, beware of falling into the trap of assuming the format as based upon the style of the event. It may be that this G&S production was set in a different place and time from the original, but the requirement for the lighting could still fall into either format. Just because a specific piece may scream out as being 'normal' and in a traditional style, doesn't instantly categorise it as requiring a traditional realistic style of lighting, and of course the reverse is the case for other less traditional works.

Your discussions with others will probably start with some major considerations of the venue that you are performing in. For many of you this may seem a silly and irrelevant issue, after all, you, your director and the rest of your production team may already know the venue, probably from many years of experience and previous productions. But at the early discussions and planning stage there may be some specific requirement that warrants discussion, because it may seriously affect your lighting. For example, within your venue, the producer or director might decide that a thrust or extended stage is needed to get the acting company closer to the audience, but what if you have no lighting positions from which to actually light this new extended stage area? I'm sure you get the idea.

For simplicity, let's assume that you are looking at just one option where the venue and its regular performance stage is concerned, more than likely somewhere you know, so all you need to establish is the style of the piece.

Decisions Concerning Style

Discussion about the style of the piece will usually spell out a number of indicators about the style of your lighting design. At this point you will probably have sketches or even a model to look at, courtesy of the set designer, or in the case of a hired-in production some photos of what the set looks like for real. Probably the most important factor regarding your lighting will be the answer to the question: "Are you looking for the 'realistic' feel or are you working at a 'surrealistic' level?" Let me offer a typical example: a pantomime production versus a straight play.

In the play, let's assume it's a box set with windows in one wall looking out onto a garden. In a night time scene you could make a case for providing no lighting at all outside the windows because when it's dark outside, it's dark, that's it. Try looking out of your window at home late at night, unless you have a street light or specific outdoor light, it's dark, so the realistic effect is to produce the same lighting state.

Now consider a night time scene in a pantomime, with probably a more or less open stage, *unlike the box set in the play*, with a painted back cloth or plain cyclorama. The 'normal' tradition would be to produce a dark blue wash for the backcloth, the surrealist interpretation of night and in this type and style of production it's what's expected.

So you can see two totally different requirements for how you may need to treat just one aspect of lighting within your production and you and the rest of the production team need to be in agreement about it all before you start getting involved in the technical planning of how you are going to make it happen.

My scenario of the pantomime versus the straight play, realism versus surrealism, and looking at only one very small aspect, the backcloth or cyclorama, is of course very over-simplified. Within the play, you may have to produce lighting to provide the transition from day to night for the exterior lighting, and in the pantomime you could have a moon on your backcloth and a need for a strong steely backlight to simulate the moonlight effect.

Design Without Artistry?

There is of course a classification of lighting design that really puts all of the decision making onto you, without the help or guidance from a production team. It may be that you are tasked to light a non-theatrical event or presentation, perhaps a product promotion, an annual sales meeting, a public speaker at an after dinner party – the list of non-theatrical lighting is endless. But in all these conditions the requirements are the same, the event or personnel require a level of illumination to accentuate the event in question. The after dinner speaker is usually not much of a problem, but some of the other events may need careful planning.

Take the annual sales meeting conference: on the face of it, it's surely not much more than one or two people standing up at a lectern and being lit while they deliver some words about sales figures to the assembled audience. Maybe, but if their oration is referenced to a Powerpoint presentation projected onto a screen standing beside them and your lighting has used the wrong equipment from the wrong positions, and light is focused all over the screen as well as the presenter, the screen images will be unreadable and your lighting has not succeeded. Even worse, it has actually detracted from the whole event.

Remember also, that in this scenario you are probably dealing with people who are not used to being lit and you could have everything set up and focused perfectly, to be greeted by cries of "I can't read my notes, those lights are in my eyes". In this case and in other non theatrical lighting there is a certain amount of education required, to be delivered by you towards the participants, in order that they understand one of the principles of lighting: that for them to be seen by others, they themselves have to endure what for some people can be an unnerving experience of 'being in the spotlight', and you might need to add for those totally unaccustomed to it, "try not to move about too much, because the lighting focused on that lectern position won't move if you do." Although of course the lighting provided will work effectively, aiding the presentation because positioned and focused correctly, it won't affect the projected image on the projection screen.

This little section carries the title *Design Without Artistry*, but you don't have to leave all your artistic talents behind, even though there may seem to be no demand from the end users. Taking our sales conference as the example, you could use the odd gobo here and there to break up the monotony of the masking flats that surround the projection screen, and if the budget will stretch that far what about the company logo made up in a custom gobo and rotating gently on the screen while the room is filling up with people? Both are relatively simple things to do and things which add that little extra to the event.

A Reality Check

Getting back to more theatrical lighting, in *Basics – A Beginner's Guide to Stage Lighting* I made reference to lighting for performance needing to be accentuated. Now even for the realistic type of lighting, you are going to produce a lighting condition, which by the nature of being in a performance space is not exactly realistic; but it needs to follow the ideas and have an end product of the realistic condition and the 'feel' that you are trying to recreate. This is perhaps the most difficult thing to do with performance lighting, for no other reason than the expectations of your audience who will all have their own interpretation and expectations of just how close to reality your efforts have been. Whereas in the realms of surrealistic and effect lighting, the concept and indeed the success of the lighting, is your own interpretation and since it never pretended to be realistic, very few people will give you an argument about how right or wrong it is, only about whether or not they liked it and if it was effective.

Within the process of design, and possibly the next step, is to have in your mind the choice and use of colour. Again, this will probably be balanced and founded by conversations and information coming from others: the director and probably the set designer and of course some of the concepts will have been set during your initial conversations about the style.

It's quite a big generalisation to make, but if you are looking at realistic works you probably won't be using very much strong and vibrant colour, and that which you do use will probably be within what I would call the pastel shades. It's equally true to say that where you are looking to use surrealistic and effect lighting, then the deeper colour shades are the norm, right up to the deep saturated colours.

Something Else to Consider

I need to make a comment at this point, that the lighting design I am talking about is for live public consumption. It's lighting for the human eye and not specifically for the film or video camera. There are two main reasons why there is a difference between lighting for the camera and lighting for your audience. Firstly, unless you are working on quite a large scale film or video recording, you will be producing your lit image for just one single reference point – one single camera lens, probably at a fixed location, rather than a seated audience of hundreds of pairs of eyes spread over the width and depth of the auditorium. Secondly, even with today's modern equipment, film, TV and video lighting in its true professional form will need to use equipment (*lanterns*) that are colour corrected. That is, the light output from them is at a level referenced to colour temperature, measured in degrees Kelvin.

This is all to do with colour balance referenced to the white colour scale, in which a higher colour temperature is used than generally found in ordinary theatre stage lighting equipment. True, in recent years the electronic ability of the camera to work well in low light conditions, and the fact that most theatre style tungsten halogen lamps now output a higher colour temperature will make it possible to achieve a reasonable level of video recording from your theatre stage performance lighting, but it's still really a different medium and I believe it's vital that you and your production team agree which is going to take precedence: the camera or your audience.

So now we're getting some of the issues of the concepts sorted out, let's assume that you are familiar with the venue you are going to work in, and that you are happy with the production style that you are going to produce the lighting for, and that there are no problems of specific film or video requirements. We seem to have been doing a lot of thinking and talking to other people, but as yet absolutely no element of design. We are getting towards the hardware but we've not quite finished with the design concepts yet.

Lanterns: Information for the First-Time Designer

Within your specific venue, you probably have an existing assembly of lanterns, or at least the positions from which to suspend and rig lanterns. Now I don't propose to go over old ground here, but if you are new to this task and if indeed this is to be your first attempt at lighting design, then you really are going to need some information on just what the lanterns can and cannot do for you. They are the tools of your trade, they are the start and almost the end of your lighting efforts. You can get some information on lanterns from *Basics – A Beginner's Guide to Stage Lighting* and probably alongside this sort of information, the very best course of action is to set aside some time to experiment with what you have and find out exactly what each lantern type will produce for you in your performance space.

This process, for the uninitiated, is a 50/50 thing: firstly the actual lantern, light output and controllability and secondly the location in which you can position it. The ability of a specific lantern type is important, but equally so is the position in which it is to be used. For the majority of lighting applications within a typical end-stage performance venue, these positions will be above and in front of the performers on stage. But how do you know how high above and how far in front? Well, as I said, your venue will probably have these factors already in place and it may not be possible to change them. If you are lucky the positions and even the lanterns provided will be more or less what's needed to provide performance lighting in your venue.

Sadly for some this will not be the case, because in many venues the quantity of lanterns and positions selected for them, will be inadequate and totally wrong for the venue. This is due to several factors such as costs and a lack of understanding of the requirements of performance lighting by those people and planners who actually put the building together. It's not surprising when you stop to consider it that in a purpose made 'theatre' style venue, where a reasonable budget was given and the requirements of the place were solely to cater for theatrical presentation works, that these places tend to work quite well. Compare this to a modern multi function (school) hall, which may have been designed to cover any number of different uses: maybe part sports hall, part flat floor general assembly place, maybe a dining hall, and alongside these requirements it also has to provide all the facilities for a performance venue.

Or maybe it's an older building that's been converted for use as a performance space, but since its original shape and use was for something different, it simply doesn't have the structural ability to provide the lighting positions required.

You will probably appreciate by now that this lighting design business really divides into two categories, one which has to utilise what exists, both venue and equipment, and one which through the available time scale and budget, can specify the level of equipment and, within reason, even change the shape and nature of the venue to suit the needs of the production and its lighting design requirements.

For many of you, I suspect the first category is where you are at. In truth this makes the lighting design job fairly simple, because there's not much to actually 'design'. Just think about it. If you have limited time and budget, you can't hope to change very much from the last efforts of either yourself or whoever had the lighting job before you, but hopefully from these few pages you will at least gain a few tips and pointers which will help you along the way.

Of course the second category is where you can give full vent to your design concepts, with plenty of time, help and budget with which to put your planning into practice. Yes it's true that there is likely to be halfway house, a crossover point, between the two categories described where you do have some opportunity and a real requirement to actually design the lighting. It may be that the group that you work with has no regular base for performance, or that the place you use has very little by way of actual equipment, so you have to bring it into the space and rig it into place for every production. There are many variations in how people have to operate and I'm conscious that I can't hope to cover all of the specific options and methods in this book. So my *Basic* offerings are often very general, but some will be common to all aspects of lighting design.

Time

Over the last page or so, I'm sure I have made three or four references to time, and this factor, even above your budget, is likely to be the deciding factor in what your design concept can actually produce. At risk of going over some old ground, I really feel it's important to make this point again. You and your production team would be best advised to adopt a professional plan, for the schedule of time and works involved, in the run up to your production or event. Let's assume it's a regular theatrical style production, as opposed to cabaret or even a sales conference.

Taken from *Basics – A Beginner's Guide to Stage Lighting:*

> *Simply work backwards from the first night/performance, filling in the known requirements: final dress, first dress, full run + technical, full run – technical, technical run, plotting, focusing. Of course you can mix and amend any of this selection to suit whatever is normal for your event. The whole point is to create a sufficient amount of 'technical' time.*

Now I know that many of you reading this, will say "We simply can't work that way, we just don't have the time available". You may even combine all of my suggested schedule into just one run through – what you probably call the dress rehearsal. All I can say is that if it works for you then fine, but I suggest that if you are going to advance your lighting performance and try to improve from previous efforts, then some of the things that you do will need more time.

You are bound to find that time is your enemy, and you never have enough of it. When you think you have everything sorted and enough time allocated, something will crop up which just proves you wrong. Simply put, your lighting can't 'perform' if you haven't had enough time to put it all in place. It's no different from the acting company not having the time to learn their lines and your results with the lighting performance will be just as catastrophic.

Your Concepts

When you analyse what you are going to do in the design process, you will find that is breaks down into several considerations, which will all interact, coming together to produce the lighting element of your production. You, as the individual responsible, will soon realise that you will fall into one of two categories.

1 That you know what you want it to look like, but have little or no ability to make the technical things come together to actually make it happen.

2 That you have the technical know-how, but lack the guidance, knowledge, experience or even just the imagination, to decide just what it should look like.

I suspect that for lots of people, you start off as a member of the second category, then you gradually learn how to use the technical knowledge to the requirements of lighting the production. There are of course some people who may start this way, but never really evolve into a lighting designer. They may be destined for a different challenge, probably as a director, which may explain why you will find some directors who have a need to be very involved with the lighting of the production, even regarding it as a vital and integral part of the production (*which I believe it is*) while some directors give little thought to the lighting, content that the acting company can carry the whole event, and be happy to accept (*almost*) whatever lighting is offered.

So what of these considerations? Well, as I said earlier, your design ideas, that mind's eye vision of what you want, is all very well but is it realistically achievable within your timescale and budget? It may be a good concept, but if it stands no chance of happening you are wasting your time and effort. When working with your conceptual ideas that you are confident can be achieved, don't forget to include the actions and abilities of your fellow workers in your planning.

Yes, it may be that your design can be achieved, but if it calls for a level of programming (at the lighting control desk) or even just in the operation that makes it impractical, again you could be wasting your time. That is, if the lighting control desk were an old preset type, then successive rapid lighting cues (lighting changes) simply may not be achievable because of lack of time to make the necessary presets, whereas a memory lighting desk has no such limitations, as the preset changes are held within the desk's memories and are accessed as fast as you can press a button.

A Conceptual Exercise

There are countless ways in which your conceptual ideas and ideals may be turned into reality, questioned and modified in order to achieve a compromise, or of course discarded altogether as being totally impractical. Try a little experiment with the following scenario:

Without for a moment getting involved with the technical schedule or layout of the equipment (lanterns) consider and roughly describe to yourself the main features of lighting for Act 1 of Puccini's La Bohème. The setting (in its traditional location) is a garret apartment with a rooftop view over Paris. One of the main features of the set is a large skylight window, since one of the most famous arias in the entire opera repertoire 'Your Tiny Hand is Frozen' takes place towards the end of this act, within which there is reference to moonlight. That should give you at least one clue about a prime requirement. There is also quite a bit of business to do with a stove, usually sitting in the middle of the set and there are references to it being cold inside the room. The whole feel of the room is intended to look and feel rather austere. The piece was written in 1896 and tells the story of a group of students, particularly Rudolfo and Mimi, and the work is classified as a tragic opera. So stop here, take a few minutes to create a picture in your mind, before you read on. Then we'll see if you and I agree about some of the concepts.

OK, here goes. I would think of it in realistic (*that's accentuated realistic*) terms, the reference to the stove in the room and specific mention of it being cold, would lead me to think of a two colour (one warm one cold) coverage and of course that moonlight just has to be there as it's actually described in the singing. More information is needed concerning the stove. Yes, it may well need to be practical with a light source inside it, but does it need to have a lighting coverage to mimic the warm glow coming from it or is the practical effect enough in itself? The director should give guidance on this. The moonlight is an interesting issue, some may say that it is an effect and by accentuating it quite a lot, in fact making a feature of it, you might argue that it's effect lighting and here I am saying that I regard the lighting for this piece as realistic. I suggest that this is regarded in another way. I have used the phrase before; it's not so much effect lighting, as *effective* lighting, and for me they are not the same thing.

How did you get on, anywhere near my thoughts? Thinking about the concepts and going back to consider that moonlight, it will probably require a fair degree of time, equipment and effort to make it work, but it's a 'must have', not an option to be downgraded.

Expectations

There is one thing that I suggest you need to get clear in your own mind during any design process, and this is probably most relevant to the realistic style of lighting. That is your own expectation of what you will produce as a piece of lighting work. Yes, I described it as a 'piece of work' just as a composer would regard their music, or indeed a performer would regard their characterisation of a specific role. The lighting, its brightness and darkness, its colour or lack of it, its movement in transition from one lighting condition to another, its ability to work in sympathy with the actions of the piece of theatre being performed, all this and much more, is just as much a performer as the set, costumes, and, dare I even suggest, the acting company.

It's at this point that you need to pause to consider just how you will feel about it and why the realistic style will probably differ from all others, because in your efforts to provide realism, you are inevitably trying to make the lighting just as ordinary and un-noticeable as possible. Probably the very best compliment you can ever have for your lighting in this style, is that "it wasn't noticed". If you achieve this, be happy in yourself that you have got it right and don't worry about the lack of plaudits for your efforts that have seemingly gone unnoticed.

While I'm on this subject, there is of course the other end of the spectrum – please excuse the lighting connection pun – where your lighting is likely to play a more active role in the performance. For in surrealistic or effect lighting, the lighting you create is meant to be noticed, it's loud, it's brash, it's in your face, it's an integral part of the performance; so much so that a realistic approach to lighting would look wrong and get noticed for its poor contribution to the overall event. Now here you would be almost disappointed if your lighting didn't get at least a complimentary mention.

I suppose I should dedicate at least a whole chapter at this point, to the un-sung heroes of performance theatre – the lighting designers – who by and large, get very little credit for their creativity, not to mention their burnt fingers, bleeding knuckles, lack of sleep and torn out locks of hair that bring about a vital part of any performance. Somehow they always seem to be way down the list when the performance was a success. Strangely the reverse is true if things didn't go too well. But no, I don't need to waste a whole chapter on these feelings here. For those of you who have tried lighting design, you know all this already and for those of you who are new to it all, you will find out soon enough!

Equipment in Your Thoughts and Planning

We have been discussing the attributes of various lanterns and the importance of their location and I expect you might wonder why I have made no specific mention of the modern move to use automated lanterns? There are two main reasons. Firstly, for lighting in the realistic category, apart from the labour saving aspects of the actual machinery – there being little or no requirement for hands-on focusing once the things are rigged in place – you probably don't actually want to use the primary attribute associated with them: their ability to move. Secondly, the cost of the equipment which is usually prohibitively expensive, costing on average ten times that of a fixed focusing lantern (although the prices are falling rapidly), coupled with which is the fact that they will require a slightly different technical treatment in their power supplies, their control desk and its operation, and not forgetting the level of technical competence needed to get the best results from them. Don't misunderstand me, I applaud the technology and the dynamic dimension which they bring to your lighting when you need it, but let's face it, they are anything but *basic*, so on the costs and technology alone, I'm not going to major their use in my thoughts on helping you with the basics of lighting design.

To conclude the conceptual part of your design, there are a few other elements which, although they are practical matters, you can't ignore from your concepts. These are the dimmers and control systems, which give you the ability to vary the intensity of your lighting and achieve changes that may be either subtle and delicate, or harsh and instant. Within this you will need to consider:

a) what you *have* to work with.
b) what you would *like* to work with, and
c) what you *need* to work with.

If you are lucky, what you actually end up with won't adversely affect your concepts too much. That is, you will have enough dimmer channels to support the quantity of lanterns needed, and the control desk will be able to cope with your demands (probably being a desk with a memory function) *including the ability of the operator*.

Something both you and the others involved in your production should remember are the evolutionary changes in the lighting of a performance event. The technological advances that have come to us in the last 25 years or so have been quite staggering, and in performance lighting we have come a long way in a very short time.

This isn't going to be history story, well not much, but when I was working at The Hippodrome Theatre in Birmingham in the early 1970s the dimmer board was a wire-wound resistance Strand Grand Master with 64 dimmers. For those that don't know, these things were massive mechanical constructions, that often took two or three people to operate. A refit during the late 1970s and then again in the1980s saw the dimmers change to a more modern electronic component type and increase to 120, then 240 in number, being controlled by a memory lighting desk; and in 2002 the most recent refit increased the dimmers to almost 500 with status reporting to a more comprehensive memory control desk.

The same thing, to some degree, has been going on in many performance spaces all over the country, all of which brings about a bigger, better, brighter end product. I suspect that a few of you may still be stuck in a 20th century time warp, never having had the benefit of many, or *even any*, of the new technologies. The real problem is that for those whose technology has stood still, their expectations probably have not. The consequence of this is that some of you will be expected to produce the 21st century end product, but only be able to use 20th century tools. You don't need to be a genius to realise that this isn't likely to work and of course there's no magic answer to it, except money and time, – but if you find yourself in this situation, be aware of the pitfalls and traps that await you. The biggest and worst of all is to get carried away with a few sparkling effects, while the overall lighting is poor and patchy. This brings me to describe and discuss in more detail one of my 'must have' things in lighting design – the lighting coverage.

2 PRACTICAL MATTERS

So Where are Your Lanterns?
Positions and Angles

Remember I made reference to lanterns being above and in front of the performer? Well that's rather a simple and not wholly accurate statement. If you are looking at a traditional end stage, proscenium arch style venue, then as a general statement it's about right, although for many other styles of performance venue, it's not quite that simple.

I'm likely to start making some more general statements in this chapter, some of which may cause you to question my advice. Please try to remember that these generalisations are hardly the cast-in-stone rules of lighting design, but they are things which I have found work to good effect.

In lighting the performer, the angle from the performance floor to the luminaire (lantern) should be between 45° to 65° and be approximately 45° to left and right. In practice what I am describing is two light sources, at 45° to left and right, and not less than 45° elevation in front of the performer.

As I've said, I am using a large generalisation here: 45° to 65° and two light sources. Let me deal with the angle first. When considering the human face, indeed the whole human form, including clothing, under normal lighting requirements you will need to provide a light source that lights your subject so that the seated audience has a view which is not adversely affected by the lighting. In other words it should look normal, *remembering my comments about having to accentuate things a little in performance lighting.*

Well if the angle of the light is too steep, then the forehead and eyebrows will put the eye sockets into shadow, making your subject appear to have very dark eyes. If the angle is too shallow, then the light may take away the natural light and shade aspects of the face, making it appear flat and lifeless. Worse still, after your light has lit its intended target, you are left with the shadow to cope with.

Then there's my comment about using two light sources, at 45° left and right of the performer. I hope that we can agree that for a large amount of general lighting requirements, your subject would look rather odd, if only lit from one light source position and of course the complete arrangement of performance lighting will almost certainly provide lighting for your subject from a number of different angles, not simply 45° in front and above from two light sources. But back to *Basic* principles, you have to learn to walk before you can run, so for starters, let's stick with my suggestion that your performer will need to be lit by two light sources (lanterns) being positioned as described. Remember also that in this scenario we are lighting for an end stage environment.

Quite often, the lighting we are trying to achieve on the performance stage is a cross between portrait photography and something seen in reality. Well in truth it's nowhere near the delicacy of the portrait photograph (although sometimes it can get close) and of course our strivings to achieve realism, as I have said, are open to a wide individual range of interpretation and acceptance. And all this is coupled with that accentuation for the stage that I keep mentioning.

In *Basics – A Beginners Guide to Stage Lighting* I described the process involved in lighting the performance stage and made reference to what I described as a two colour three area coverage. This is not my invention; I know that many lighting designers use this general area coverage, so I'm certainly not making any claims to inventing anything, but I do know that it works for lots of performance lighting requirements.

This small section started off talking about lighting the performer, as in one artiste, but now I have started talking about a two colour area coverage, how does this tie together? Simple really, once you take on board the principle behind it all.

A group of lanterns focused onto individual areas of the performance stage for a specific effect may not be able to provide an even overall coverage of light, but the focus of lanterns into an even overall coverage will probably be able to provide the individual areas' coverage.

These suggestions about lantern positions and angles are generalisations and yes I know, before you feel the urge to write and tell me, it doesn't cover all the requirements of lighting design – there's more to come later – but this is *Basics* and as I've said, for lots of applications, my basic generalisations will work.

A Focus Coverage

For those who didn't read *Basics – A Beginners Guide to Stage Lighting,* the following section describes what the three area two colour coverage is all about.

Taken from *Basics – A Beginners Guide to Stage Lighting:*
Divide the stage into three areas: left, centre and right. Remember we are dealing in stage technical terms, stage left being actor's left when looking into the auditorium. It matters very little, if at all, about the size of the stage because if you are dealing with a large stage you are likely to be working with 1.2 or 2kW lanterns which are working over quite a long throw (distance) whereas on a small stage you may be working with 500 or 650W lanterns working over a much shorter throw. The end result is that the light output in area coverage will be similar. You could of course divide the stage area into four or five areas but let's start with the regulation three.

Assume there is an over stage lighting bar directly upstage of the main house tabs and this is populated with 12 lanterns (Fresnels) spaced evenly within the proscenium opening. Starting at the stage left end of the bar focus the first lantern almost straight down, making a coverage of the downstage left area. Then focus the third lantern linking to the first, so covering downstage centre, and then the fifth linking to cover downstage right. Now simply mirror this focus with lanterns seven (down left), nine (down centre) and eleven (down right). You now have the three stage areas lit from two positions (angles), and of course if you have achieved the coverage trick the whole of the down stage front area should be evenly lit from left to right.

But we started off with 12 lanterns! What about the other six? OK. Now this is the really cleaver bit – but first you have to take on board just a little design concept.

Most stage lighting requirements will call for at least a two colour coverage: one in a warm colour, one in a cold colour. This simple statement could take at least a whole chapter to discuss and disseminate and probably will cause much comment along the lines of: "How boringly ordinary", "Not in this production", etc, etc. But remember the aims of my comments are to provide the beginner with a basic level of information and advice, and my advice is that "Most stage lighting requirements will call for at least a two colour coverage".

So, back to our other six lanterns. You probably won't be surprised that they should focus in exactly the same positions as the first six, but this now provides the opportunity for a second colour coverage.

Our first bar of 12 lanterns will of course be duplicated at a front-of-house position and at further overstage positions, continuing the coverage and extending it to cover as much of the stage area as required. It is quite normal for two or even three more bars of lanterns to be rigged and focused in this way.

For the purpose of our exercise we will use a pale straw or amber for one colour coverage and a pale steel blue or steel tint for the other. What this actually provides you with is a very powerful tool in the stage lighting armoury: the ability to light an area of the stage in either colour from either side.

Picture our proscenium stage complete with a box set (scenery forming the walls of a room starting at down stage left and running up stage, across stage and down to stage right). Let's assume there is a large French window in the stage left wall of the set, being the main source for 'natural daylight' into the room/set.

Now if we use as the strongest light source all of our lanterns positioned on stage left, i.e. lanterns 1-3-5 from our first overstage bar in the warm (pale straw or amber) coverage and complement this with lanterns 8-10-12 in the cold (pale steel blue/tint) coverage, the effect this will have on the performers is that on one side (stage left where the light is supposed to be coming from) they will be lit with a warm colour representing and complementing the natural daylight, while on the other side the coverage will be colder, representing the darker and almost reflected light.

This is a very simple example and in real stage conditions there is quite a lot more to it than that, but I hope you get the idea of what is possible. Yes, you may argue that if you are trying to create reality it just doesn't look like that. Well may be, maybe not. Remember, you have to accentuate just a little for the stage and of course depending upon the nature and style of the production you will choose either a subtle or a vibrant range of colour.

This basic two colour multi-area coverage is of course only the start. I have not mentioned specifically the need for back light, side light, or in the case of the scenario of the box set, a large amount of light off stage focused through those French windows for effect.

I can hear you all moaning that my ideas and suggestions are way above your normal methods, because you just don't have the equipment and just how long will it take to focus! The whole idea is ridiculous, you may say.

Yes, I know that, but (and it's not a solution) when you go to see a production in a professional theatre that does have the facilities, the time and the budget, that's how it's done and albeit on a smaller scale how do you expect your production to contain similar results if you don't strive to do the same? As I said, it's not a solution, and for some it is perhaps a glimpse of Utopia.

I hope that you have managed to visualise the lighting conditions described with the warm and cool colours, the angles, the performance stage split into three distinct areas but the lighting working as an overall coverage. It might be easier to provide a shaded drawing or a photograph, but I think it's better that you have to use your imagination, putting your own visualisation onto my narrative.

Perhaps you are starting to think, "this is getting way above the level at which I have to work. All this talk about a three-area two-colour coverage, just look at the quantities of equipment involved and the time it will take." So getting down to the real *basic* level, let's just concentrate on the really important points.

1) Concentrate on an even area coverage, even if only in one colour and cover each area from two positions, providing a front lit coverage to your audience.

2) If you can identify the specific requirement, you may be able to cover the area warm form one side and cold from the other. Just remember that's what you will have for every lighting state, but if it works for you, then fine.

3) Consider those angles, too shallow or too steep and you are creating problems for yourself.

So much written down and thus far these three little notes are, you might think, just about the only information that I have offered and of course they don't give anything like the full picture of lighting for your event. True, the coverage from the correct angles will light your performers, but in order to give some depth to the picture you are painting, it's likely to need something else.

The light and shade aspects of your performer lit even by just two lanterns at 45° angles can be made by the intensity of one or both of the lanterns, even when they are in the same colour. It's rather a large step to delve into the practical matters of dimming control just at this point, because there are lots of other design concepts and other technical issues to cover first. But the actions of dimming control can, and will be, a critical factor in your lighting design, and not just because of the 'controllability' that it provides, but because in itself it will be a part of the colour rendering process that you will need to consider and use to control the lighting condition you are looking to achieve.

More Coverage

The depth that I mentioned will come from other lanterns, positioned to the side and probably above and behind your performer: sidelight and backlight. In some ways it may seem that I am advocating even more equipment in order to light your performer correctly. Well yes, but not necessarily in the quantities that you might think.

Take side-lighting. Lanterns positioned left or right of your performer, or both left and right and at a much shallower angle, will indeed light your performer from the side and with a small bonus, for lanterns at these positions will of course cover more or less every position across the stage area. You will need to be aware that where your performer moves closer to these lantern positions, the coverage that they produce will diminish, to a point where too close to the lantern will either provide no coverage at all, or possibly worse, produce an embarrassing 'hot spot' on your performer. To resolve this problem, and it's not always the complete solution, is to provide two lanterns from each side to produce your side lighting. One is probably a profile or maybe a PC with barn door, sited above head height (nominally 2.5 > 3m above floor level) giving a coverage from about centre stage off to the opposite side. The second lantern, probably a Fresnel, sited at about head height (nominally 2m above floor level) will then cover the area of performance floor nearest to itself. The focus of these two lanterns will produce an elongated coverage of light, crossing the performance space. Of course, as I noted, this coverage may be a requirement for both sides, thus four lanterns in total and yes, you guessed it, if you find you need a two colour coverage, all that will double.

This side lighting element may be fairly simple to achieve in productions using an open stage, but may not be possible at all where you are dealing with other staging formats, e.g. a box set on a proscenium stage.

Just a final point on side lighting: within dance performance work, side lighting is an absolute 'must have'. It is perhaps the most important element of lighting in this particular art form and it needs to go right down to floor level. Indeed so different is the lighting process for dance that it's almost a speciality in its own right, but being *Basics*, I won't dwell on this too much. The best advice I can give is to try to see a properly lit dance production, not to copy and mimic, but just so that you can see the dynamics of the performers and the performance space to be lit.

We seem to be going round in circles don't we? First I give you advice about why you need something and how to do it, then comes the part that says, "but it's all too much", and I will then counter that by suggesting you take just the basic principle on board, for instance use just two lanterns and a single colour coverage. The truth is that you and your requirements coupled with your technical and probably financial ability, will ultimately make the decision about just how many lanterns you are going to use. Let's face it, you are not likely to have a free hand when it comes to just how much equipment you can use to light your production and as you can probably imagine, I will confirm that no matter how much equipment you have at your disposal, you will always say you could use more.

Examples

At this point, let me describe just two actual practical examples of lighting design, one that I experienced first hand and one that I was responsible for.

1. Some years ago (back in the 1970s) while working as chief electrician at a Midlands theatre, a production by a local amateur company came into the theatre. Now the norm in this case had previously been to rely on the resident staff to provide the lighting design. However on this occasion I was advised that the company in question had secured the services of a lighting designer who worked in the television industry. Fine, an easy week for me, someone else can do all the brainwork and make the decisions about the lighting. What transpired was what I would describe as a lighting disaster. The TV lighting designer, never having worked in a theatre, did indeed design the lighting for the show. He provided a rig plan, a colour call and in the prescribed time, was in charge of the focus and plotting of the lighting. The end product was a series of brilliantly lit small areas of the stage, with the acting company moving between them in virtually no light at all. What he had designed for was lighting in a TV studio and specific camera shots, with absolutely no thought about the overall look of the complete stage.

2. Some years later, while working as the chief electrician and resident lighting designer for the Welsh National Opera, I designed the lighting for a production of Verdi's *Otello*, the final scene taking place in the bedchamber where Otello murders Desdemona. I think the overall lighting for the scene used no more than about 12 lanterns in total and all but one were a part of the two-colour three-area coverage which I described earlier. At least one newspaper critic was moved to mention the "superb dark intensity" of the lighting in the last scene.

These two examples, prove or possibly disprove, what I am trying to flag up for your attention: the fact that the area coverage of lighting for your stage can be made to work in lots of different ways. However, to forgo the even overall coverage may have seriously detrimental effects on your production.

It's also a fact often discussed amongst the lighting designer fraternity, that results and effectiveness don't automatically require vast amounts of equipment. True, the 'saturation rig' approach will probably provide more opportunities to light your subject in different ways, but simply to have more, to make the overall lighting simply brighter, is no guarantee that it will make it 'better'. Indeed too much light in almost any given lighting requirement can sometimes prove a distraction to your audience, so even if you are fortunate enough to have volumes of equipment at your disposal don't rush to use it all at once.

More Details on the Lighting Coverage

Thinking about my proposed use of that three-area two-colour coverage, what I am advocating is the controlled use of small areas of light, focused together to bring about a wider coverage of the area. For the beginner you could argue that a similar coverage could be achieved by using fewer lanterns, but by spreading the area coverage of each. The problem with this is that you simply won't have the intensity in any given (smaller) area when you need it. So the theory of my argument is to provide enough equipment to give the controlled area coverage, but stopping well short of that saturation rig that I spoke about.

I expect the next question you may have, if you plan to use the three-area two-colour coverage, is just how you provide lighting for those special little areas and positions that will crop up in most productions? Well not unsurprisingly, more lanterns, let's call them 'specials' for no other reason than the name fits, for when the overall coverage doesn't quite do the job, or there is a specific need, then it's a special requirement. Some productions may call for quite a few specials, some hardly any. Your assessment of their requirements will usually come from a combination of watching rehearsals, studying the set (model or plan) and of course talking with the director and others in the design team in those early planning days, because you really don't want to find out about a special requirement after you have rigged and focused everything. Of course you may have the option of using perhaps the ultimate special: the followspot, but I'll have a lot more to say about that later on.

There is another factor in your lighting design which really shouldn't be a consideration within the design at all; it's really more to do with the direction of the piece rather than the design of the lighting, and I suppose technically it's as much to do with the focus of the lanterns as anything else. This is the ability of your acting company to deliver their most important lines of the whole show from the one place on the stage where you have not provided adequate lighting coverage. Believe me, they will do it. Over the years I've come to name it as 'proscenium arch acting'. It's usually prevalent in non-professional productions or events where the performers appear to be stage shy, not wanting to occupy the front and centre positions, but cling like limpets to the extremities of the stage. You may have sat through rehearsals and watched the director giving them specific positions and movements, known as 'blocking', but when they get on stage, the magnetic attraction of the prosc arch will drag them over to it, to a point just where your lighting does not quite cover. Well there are two solutions to this. Obviously you can mention it to the director who could have a word with the acting company, but maybe your best course of action is to be critical with your focus, and of course to use the correct lanterns from the correct positions to provide the lighting coverage.

The 'Critical Focus'

I have to go over some old ground here, in what I call 'The Critical Focus', and if there was ever one golden rule in lighting design, it would be this. *"Get the focus right, because lanterns focused in the wrong place simply can't do the job."* We'll forgo, but not forget, the part about getting the lanterns in the right position. I'll come back to this, but what I'm talking about here is the actual mechanical hands-on focusing of the lantern. I've called the lanterns your tools; they are first and foremost what does the lighting job and your operation, your ability, your patience and understanding of the mechanical and human requirements within the focusing process, is absolutely vital.

Taken from *Basics – A Beginners Guide to Stage Lighting*:

> *The performance area dark and quiet, personnel in place, off we go (at last) so what do you do? What do you say? First call for the dimmer channel controlling the lantern to be focused and if you are lucky the thing will actually come on. If it doesn't? Well that's another chapter; let's assume it works!*
>
> *The act of focusing for the person on the ground is mostly a matter of personal preference. Some people will stand where they want the lantern to*

focus and look directly at the lantern and give instructions to the focuser. Some prefer to view the result from a distance, again giving instructions. Probably the most popular method is to stand in the position where the lantern is to be focused but with your back to the lantern so that you can see the light output on the floor with your shadow in it. One slight draw back to this is that you are now facing away from the person at the top of the ladder doing the hands-on work, so the instructions should be clear and loud – often accompanied by hand movements – telling the focuser left, right, up, down, larger, smaller and any actions required for barndoors or shutters.

Some people prefer to focus a lantern in white light, adding colour only when the final position has been set. Others prefer the colour to be applied from the start of the process. Whatever the choice, the most important thing is that at the end of the focus the lantern is locked tight in position, both pan and tilt. Of course, this action is made by the focuser, but the person on the ground should be satisfied that the locking off is complete. Don't be in too much of a hurry to speed your focuser onto the next lantern – remember it can be a difficult task at the top of a ladder in the semi-dark working with a hot lantern, especially at 2am when you are tired and have the prospect of several more hours of being shouted at from below. Indeed, if the focusing session is for a large rig of lanterns the hands on focusing should be rotated in shifts if at all possible.

Experience and practice will of course help, and it is often found that when a designer (on the ground giving instructions) works regularly with a focuser, an understanding will grow between the two, sometimes to the point where very little is said and with most actions happening almost automatically with a few hand gestures.

So you have focused a lantern and going back to our coverage we need to focus the next one. You will need to leave on the first lantern, possibly at a reduced light level, so that you can see where its coverage ends. It's then a relatively simple task to overlap the next lantern. Don't forget the cone effect and that at actor's head height the coverage will be smaller than it appears on the performance floor.

During this process you will find it useful to walk through the combined area of the two lanterns at the overlap position. Use your rig plan/clip board or simply the back of your hand to test and assess the meld between the lanterns making the coverage. This way, if you have any little holes in your coverage you can make adjustments.

I'm sure you have spotted that this last section – about the actions of the focus – is talking about several people being involved. You the designer, there is the focuser with hands on the lanterns, and probably someone at the lighting control desk to actually turn on the dimmer channel. Apart from the numbers of people involved, the other things vital to the focus session are a blackout and a relatively quiet area. Where you are going to focus lanterns onto a specific position, you can't do it accurately in bright working light conditions with lots of other people running around performing other technical tasks on stage.

I know that for many lighting design practitioners what I'm describing in this critical focus may be way above your 'normal' operating method and I can't offer much by way of a practical solution in this. It may seem a giant step for those of you who fall into this category, but consider this. Remember I've said that it's simply not possible to give you a list of how to design lighting and that some of the things contained in this book may help you to some degree. Well, getting the critical focus right is probably the most important factor of all and if you don't have the dedicated time and are forced to work in less than ideal conditions, you aren't likely to advance your lighting very much from your previous efforts. If you are a first time designer, I suggest that you start as you intend to continue and spell it out to the others in your production team that this issue of critical focus needs just as much dedicated time as the set construction or acting company rehearsals. If they disagree tell them to phone me for some candid words of advice!

For the beginner, this topic of critical focus has another vital element. Actually it's really very closely linked to my recommendations for the lighting coverage, but it's summed up in the statement that says, "don't just concentrate on lighting the floor", and to understand the meaning of this, the beginner needs to remember what they are dealing with. When the light leaves your lantern and is focused down onto the stage, the shape of the beam of light is a cone. As it hits the stage floor, depending upon the angle, being directly overhead (90°) or off to one side (45°), the coverage provided will be either a regular circle or an ellipse. Now mindful of my comments and requirements to provide that seamless coverage, you might expect to overlap the edges of these multiple light outputs. Quite right, but likely as not you will just have made the most basic of beginners' mistakes, for in doing this what you have done is to light the floor, but the cone shape of the beam of light does not cover the same area at the important position, 1-2 metres above the floor – this being exactly where the important upper half of your acting company will be.

ensure that even coverage at the head high position above the stage floor. That's why I made reference to checking the coverage with your clipboard, or the back of your hand.

In this typical example of lighting the floor but not the actor, you can see also the relevance of the positioning of lanterns in the right place. As I said, it's a 50/50 thing. Yes, the critical focus has to be correct, but then so does the position of the lantern. I know I'm repeating myself but I can't stress enough just how important and critical this will be to your lighting efforts.

The Standard Rig and Focus

For those of you new to lighting design, where you are working in a known space having existing lighting positions and equipment (lanterns) already rigged, you may find that almost by default your predecessors and the venue have put in place what many people call the 'standard rig'. This will probably provide what may be regarded as the standard focus, hopefully producing something near to my suggestions for the three-area two-colour coverage. Remember that I made a reference to this almost right at the start, making the comment that in this case there isn't much to actually 'design'. Indeed, some might suggest that the standard rig and focus really isn't part of your design at all, it's just the staring point, the clean sheet of paper, on which you will draw your picture with light. I don't subscribe to this view; I suggest that the standard focus is every bit as important as anything else you do in providing the overall lighting for a production.

If you find yourself working within the confines of a standard rig and focus, I suggest that you shouldn't be in too much of a hurry to change it without first having a look at the end product of what's actually in place. You might find you can make use of it, even if you have to tweak the focus and extend it a little here and there. If the person who put it in place is on site and available, talk over your requirements with them – a little cooperation could save both parties quite a lot of work. Anyway the time factor (and the budget) may dictate what you can do. Don't forget that many places that have adopted the standard rig and focus have done so for very good reasons. It may be a venue that has to cater for many and various different events and production styles, taking place in a relatively short space of time – so much so that there simply won't be the time to achieve any radical changes to put your rig and focus ideas into place. And don't forget that when your event is over the venue probably needs to return to its original rig and focus.

Real Practical Matters

At this point and moving on to the actual equipment involved, we could get rather hijacked by the technical issues involved in the preparation and rigging process, so I'll try to make this section brief.

It might seem a blindingly obvious point to make, but since it involves not wasting that precious time you don't have enough of, when rigging lanterns, make sure that they actually work before you rig them into position! I don't just mean the lamp – all aspects of the lantern's operating functions need to be checked, i.e. the focus adjustment within your Fresnels, PCs and profiles (for profiles it's the flat field or peak adjustment and the focus adjustment of the lens or lenses) the free running rotation of any barndoor units fitted to Fresnels and PCs, and within those profiles, the action of the masking shutters, for stiff and ceased up shutters are a real pain and you can bet that if the profile you're are working with is missing a shutter altogether, it will be the one you need most in the focus process. Lastly, don't ignore the hook clamp or other means of suspending the lantern – plus the lantern's safety bond. Five minutes spent in checking these things at ground level can save you hours if you are forced to undertake a repair once rigged.

In preparation for the focus session you will hopefully have settled on your selection of colour. I say hopefully because especially for the first time designer, when you actually see the outcome of your colour selection you might feel that some changes are needed. I think this is rather inevitable, because looking at a likely colour choice in isolation by leafing through a colour sample book and holding your selection up to a light, is never quite the same as the actual colour effect produced from a group of lanterns. Not to discount the vast range and choice of colour available to you, but I think you will find that most lighting designers have their own favourite pallet of colours which they are happy to use again and again. That's not to say that their lighting is always the same, all of us will experiment and refine our choice in such things as we become more adept and used to them, but still there will be that hard core of colour choice that some people feel comfortable with.

Colour

For many years, when asked, I have fought shy of giving information on colour selection, always saying that I regarded it as a very personal thing and that anyway everyone has their own ability to actually 'see' colour in a different way.

But since this book is dealing with design concepts, I will relent, and for what it's worth, provide my favoured selection of colours and split them into two categories, the pastels and the others.

From the Lee Colour range: Pastel shades (# number reference)
#103   #109   #110   #117   #136   #138   #147   #151   #152   #159
#202   #203

Other Colours (# number reference)
#101   #102   #106   #111   #115   #119   #124   #132   #134   #141
#148   #161   #164   #180   #181

From the Rosco Supergel Colour range: Pastel shades (# number reference)
#01   #04   #05   #07   #09   #11   #13   #337   #351   #61   #66

Other Colours (# number reference)
#19   #20   #21   #339   #344   #370   #90

It's quite a lot you may think – some 45 in total – and maybe I've missed one or two. In fact you could refine this selection down to my absolute 'must have' list of less than 20, and of course in any given production it's rather unlikely you would want or need to use 40+ different colours, although I believe quite a few people would make a strong argument about that! But when you look and consider the vast choice available just from these two manufacturers, you might question just why there are so many colour choices available. Well as I've said, we all see colour in slightly different ways and I am sure that many others would have their own different favourite selection.

Let's look at a few specifics in my selection, starting with the warm colours in the pastel shades, beginning from what I regard (*see*) at the palest end of the range, where #159 and #07 provide just a hint of yellow, made slightly more yellow when used with the lanterns at 70% or less than their maximum output. I would use these colours in a wash coverage, for either interior or exterior lighting.

Staying within the yellow/amber part of the range, we come to #103 and #109, both of which make it into my 'must have' 10, which is perhaps rather odd since they are so similar, yet different enough for both to be very worthwhile. There's quite a lot to be said and use made of these pale yellow/ straws, through to pale ambers; it seems an obvious and somewhat pointless comment to make but these two offer a colour rendering that you will need and really can't get from anything else. They are very useful where you are dealing with external scenes and both work really well at low intensity levels.

Then let's consider the flesh/gold moving into the pale pinks: #05 #152 #04 #01 #109. Of these #05 and #152 are perhaps my choice for wash lighting within this range and I tend to use them most when lighting interior scenes. The remainder are perhaps a little harsh for a warm coverage, but you can never rule out any particular colour because there will be a requirement for it one day in a particular place.

Which leaves us with the stronger pastels #11 #13 #110 # 337 and #147: two yellows #11 and #13, two pinks #110 and #337, and another of my 'must have' colours #147. It's a great colour, and you can do so much with it. It's a colour in its own right and fantastic when used from low angles, providing a setting sun or early sun rise effect.

In the cold pastel shades, maybe the two palest are interesting – #202 and #203 – in that they are not actually classified as a colour filter; they are 'correction' filters, used where correction or conversion of tungsten light sources to daylight are needed, in common use in the film and TV industry. But in the world of performance lighting we're not interested in conversion factors – only the colour effect. #203 being a very pale blue and #202 just a little darker, but not much. #61 and #66 offer a slightly darker shade of blue, but still quite pale, and all four of these pale blues can be used in a wash coverage, as can another on my 'must have' list, #117; this and #61 and #66 can also be very useful in providing the simulated back lighting moonlight effect, which I suggest should be selected a shade or two lighter than the cold wash coverage. You might even want to use open white light as the moonlight, where you are using a very pale cold wash coverage.

When using these delicate pastel shades, consider opposing warm and cold colours that can work together, and even complement each other. I would use #203 with #159 in a warm/cold combination, likewise #117 ad #103 and so on through the spectrum of colour.

Remembering also that when you start dealing with the more vibrant colour ranges the choice of opposing colours is obviously much wider apart and in this case the visual aspect is one of opposition rather than complementation. However, you will still find colours which go well together in opposition, because they are evenly matched. If you use one such as #181, a very dark blue, opposing #101, a bright yellow, you will find that one may overpower the other, simply because of the amount of light transmitted through the colour.

Even selecting from your favourite colour portfolio, there is still the ultimate question to be considered about just how it's going to look when taking into consideration the sets, costumes and make-up involved. Again, talk to the others in your production team; you should be able to gauge quite a lot from the sets and costumes and what you see should give you some important markers as to what colours to select. Remember that vibrant set and costume colours will stand out by themselves, even when lit in pastel colours or white light, but sometimes the use of a strong colour will really accentuate their already vibrant colours and make them stand out even more.

You will note that I have not bothered with the names of the colours. People who know and use colour on a regular basis rarely, if ever, talk about their names. The use and familiarity is such that everything is known and understood by the number only. Anyway, with reference to my comments about us all seeing things differently, a named description of a colour is not likely to be 100% helpful to you, but you should be able to pick up a colour sample book from your friendly local theatrical hardware supplier. Some manufacturers have provided options within the layout of their colour sample books, being available (for your convenience) in either numeric order, or in what is called the 'designer' edition, where the layout may seem somewhat haphazard. This stems from the old long-established and original colour media, 'Cinemoid' (*now no longer available*) and it has simply stayed with the industry ever since. Incidentally, if any of you are still using this old range of colour filter probably tucked away in countess old cardboard boxes hidden in the dark corners of the backstage technical places, then you really should make the change to one of the modern, high temperature colour filters, since the old – quite thick by comparison – filter was never intended for use with the modern tungsten halogen light sources that we use today.

Going back once again to my recommendations about the use of a two colour coverage, one warm and one cold, there is one colour within the ranges which is rather an oddity, but very useful – the pale lavender shades, i.e. Lee #136 and Rosco #351. You will find that these rather delicate shades will work in combination with the predominant warm or cold colour used in a coverage. You may find this useful where you need to highlight a specific area but retain an overall warm or cold effect.

Finally, where colour selection is concerned, there are some occasions where a frost or diffusion filter may be useful, and as with the true colour ranges, there are quite a few to choose from. But again I would suggest that just a small selection will do the job for you: from the Rosco Supergel range #114 and #119 and from the Lee Filters range #216 and #253. For the beginner you might find it difficult to know how to use a frost or diffusion filter, or even why you may need to. The clue is in the name 'diffusion', for even when using a Fresnel lantern, having a soft focus edge to the beam of light, the use of diffusion material will really disperse the light even more. It's particularly useful where you have profile lanterns with a hard edge focus that can produce a hard line of light on the face. You will also find that the use of a diffusion filter in a profile lantern (Rosco #114) can make the focus process much faster. It's a quick and easy operation to drop in a diffusion filter – the alternative is to spend time adjusting and re-adjusting the lenses, shutters and field adjustment of the lamp.

More Practical Focus Issues

In *Basics – A Beginners Guide to Stage Lighting* I made mention of your means of access (ladders) – this being of special interest to your focuser, who has to climb up them.

I'm not going to go over all that again, for fear that many pages and much of your time could be spent delving into matters of Health and Safety. But it does flag up yet again the wide difference that exists across all those tasked to do the lighting job.

I have been banging on about time, directors/procedures, schedules, the manpower involved and all that referenced to the practical matters, the focusing of your lanterns and the plotting and technical runs and rehearsals that follow. I am aware that a large proportion of you have never worked in this way and probably don't understand my incessant harping on about it. Well maybe that fact alone explains why your lighting efforts don't quite get the job done properly?

Going back to the focus of your lanterns, I'm now flagging up *ladders*, as something to be considered and you are probably thinking, *"he's really lost the plot now"*, after all, the things themselves and their use, is something most people simply take for granted. They are hardly ever a topic of conversation, unless they are missing or broken. Many of you I'm sure will actually be using the wrong type of ladder. OK, so what's the right type of ladder? The answer's easy: one that saves you time – probably an extending aluminium mast with platform mounted on wheels, and I don't mean a scaffold tower.

There is what has become an industry standard piece of equipment called a 'Tallescope' and for those who need to climb up to their lanterns, this is the very best thing to use. Scaffold towers were never intended for use in performance spaces. For one thing, they come as a kit of parts, and before you do anything you have to assemble them and we are back to Health and Safety issues again. Are you qualified to assemble a scaffold tower? Not forgetting the time it will take to actually build it, when you have it in place in your performance stage, it will take up a lot of space and in some circumstances such as a box set with furniture and set dressings, it simply won't be usable. And then when you have finished with it, you have to spend even more time dismantling it. Finally, do you have somewhere to store a quantity of aluminium frames and poles? No, for almost all performance spaces the scaffold tower is *not* what you need. Anyway if you are looking at your access in cost terms, there's hardly any difference in price between the scaffold tower and the Tallescope.

Even with the correct equipment the focus session will take a lot more of that precious time than you expect. Even where you are working in a venue with high level walkways behind each lighting bar, it's still not a speedy operation. Obviously the overall size of the event and the numbers of lanterns involved will be a major factor, but a final note on the focus procedure: don't rush it, take the time you need to get it right.

3 RELATED ISSUES

The requirements of your lighting, no matter what style you are using, will of course be bound by the set or setting. In a traditional play setting you are probably dealing with what is known as a 'box set', with the scenery forming three sides of a room, the proscenium arch opening of course being the fourth side. But here again, there is no hard or fast rule that says this is how it must be. The same play that uses the box set could be performed in a stylised form, with very little scenery and only furniture and properties in use. A pantomime or musical production will probably adopt a more open-plan for the setting, as the nature of this type of production, not being cluttered with doors, windows and set dressings, means the whole stage is the acting area and left and right stage become open access areas for the cast.

Obviously in these two formats you will need to use and position your lighting coverage differently. You will most likely find that in the box set your coverage will be made over a smaller area than for the open stage. This simply means that each individual lantern will have its coverage made tighter or opened wider to meet the needs of the setting. You might think that if you are working over the complete stage, having to provide a wider coverage you might want to use bigger lanterns with more light output because you have to the spread the light further. This is not usually the case – remember my comments about having too much light? In general you will find that if your venue uses a normal 650W or 1200W lantern range, then there is no need to move up to the next size (1200W–2000W) just because the focus range is changing.

What to Use and Where?

So how do you decide what size of lantern to use? Well, for the vast majority of you, probably more than 90%, you are going to use either a 500W/650W range of lanterns, or a 1000W/1200W range. I should explain that the older range of lanterns will be rated to use lamps of 500W or 1000W, whereas the more modern lantern ranges are designed to use the 650W or 1200W lamps, and just to complicate matters, some of the older ranges of lanterns may have been converted to use the new higher powered lamps.

Yes, size does matter; lanterns too small and thus under-powered for the size of the venue simply won't be able to provide the light intensity needed to do the job. Likewise, over-sized lanterns are a waste since you will hardly ever use them to their full capacity and they will look out of place hanging in a smaller venue. So here's another generalisation: for the smaller venue, maybe even an open plan studio space where the lighting bars or grid are no more than 4m>4.5m above the floor, then the smaller 500W/650W range of lanterns will be fine. It therefore follows that for the larger venue with lighting bars at 5m, 6m and above, you will need to move up to the larger 1000W/1200W range of lanterns.

A note of caution at this point about how you regard these lantern capacities. In the evolution of lanterns (not forgetting the lamps inside them), until quite recently we were all happy about the lantern capacity (Wattage) of what we worked with. We all knew, not surprisingly, that a 1000W lantern would out-perform a similar type of lantern only rated at 500W. This is still the case for lanterns in the flood, Fresnel, prism convex and PAR ranges. What has changed is the use of new technologies within the profile range of lanterns. The axial lamp, the dichroic reflector and the aspheric lens have combined to improve the performance of the profile lantern to a point where a 600W modern profile will out-perform the old style 1200W version. So be aware of this and be careful about the age and type of equipment being used.

My earlier reference, about distances and Wattage or capacity was made with the use of a Fresnel or prism convex lantern in mind, but as you can see from my comments about the new current ranges of profile lanterns, it would be perfectly acceptable to use the new 600W profile lanterns over a distance not recommended for the older style 500/1000W lanterns.

But just what constitutes an area coverage from an individual lantern? Well to make yet another generalisation, it shouldn't matter much what size or capacity the lantern is. The actual area coverage should be something between 2m>3m diameter; remembering that the use of at least two lanterns in any one area will hopefully give you a coverage that extends about 2.5m above the stage floor. If you can achieve this sort of coverage with the overlapping of the areas, you should be getting somewhere between 6m>8m of overall coverage. Thinking about traditional end-stage proscenium style theatre venues, this will, I suggest, equate to the majority of proscenium arch openings that you will encounter; a good number will be considerably less, so your three area coverage should work in your venue. Yes there will be exceptions, where the venue has a very wide auditorium and thus proscenium, but even in these places the confines of the actual set stage are often made within a false proscenium (usually black masking flats or a movable, adjustable proscenium arch) so the practice of the three area coverage will probably still work.

What Dimmers and Control can do for You

You will no doubt expect that whatever the configuration and focus of lanterns used to light your production, they will all be controlled via dimming circuits. This is a somewhat contradictory act on your part, for having gone to all the time and trouble to put lanterns in place it seems a rather backward step to limit the amount of light below their maximum output. This aspect of stage lighting is an important and vital part of your design, so let me explain why.

For a start, the process of turning on each lantern or combined group of lanterns, thus achieving a lighting state starting from a blackout, is most often required to happen as a gradual fade, not an instant snap on – although of course this can be a requirement in some cases. The fade can be any duration of your choice, from two or three seconds to five or ten minutes. Having established your lighting state, sooner or later you will need to change and modify it. The transition from one state to the next is again normally made over a timed duration. Sometimes so slowly that the audience is never aware that it's happening, there being a seamless transition from one lighting state to the next with the lighting being a key factor in focusing the attention of the audience upon what the director and the actions of the piece are intending them to concentrate. Then there are occasions where the lighting change has to be made with immediate effect: e.g. when someone switches on a light switch, or simply when the action calls for an instant effect.

These are the control functions of the dimmers in your lighting system, coupled to the lighting control desk which controls them. However, just as important as the ability to control your lanterns, making changes in a timing of your choice is the ability that the dimmers provide to set the intensity of your lanterns, because this is a vital part of the balance, the tone, the depth of each lighting state that you create. Your lighting would lose an integral part of its character if all the lanterns were used at the same intensity.

This element of your lighting is where you bring all the component parts together. Having got the lanterns in the correct positions and angles, focused them correctly to cover the intended areas, and having selected the correct colour, the final piece of the jigsaw is to use the dimming and control system to set the level of the lanterns to produce the desired effect. Sounds quite simple doesn't it?

So to make your lighting really work, the ability to use less rather than the maximum available will be an important factor in your lighting. You may find that some particular production styles will indeed call for the use of the maximum available amount of light in almost all lighting states, while in other styles you may hardly ever use your lanterns at their full potential.

Harping back to my comments about having too much light, during my time as chief electrician and resident lighting designer at The Welsh National Opera, way back in the 1970s, I remember well the chief electrician at The New Theatre in Cardiff, who used to make reference to most of the operas being lit in a blackout. What a lovely Welsh phrase, and to prove the point, each time the opera came into the theatre (for a spring and autumn two- or three-week season each year) he would change all the lamps in the Fresnel lanterns on the number one bar over-stage (just about the only lanterns from the theatre that the opera company used, being more or less self-contained with lighting equipment) changing them from the usual 1000W and replacing them with a 750W version.

We were all in on the joke, but we didn't mind, because of course he was right. When dealing with a more or less completely open stage to light, the lighting state would probably be built starting from the number one bar over-stage, providing the remaining stage coverage as required. So if the lanterns in use in this position were ever called for at their maximum, which was a fairly rare event, then everything else used would balance and compensate the intensity of their output. For almost all guest lighting designers and certainly for all of the directors and producers, when the dimmer channel was at maximum that was it, obviously the lanterns couldn't be any brighter: "they're on at full" with never a thought that they were actually using under powered lamps! This little practical joke which started out simply to prove a point, became a secret tradition which to my knowledge went on for several years, and it proves the point I'm making about too much light for it's all totally relevant to the overall balance that you will create with your lighting.

So the dimmers and the control system are indeed another very important tool within the many items of hardware and sometimes slight-of-hand trickery that you will use in creating your lighting design.

I said somewhere previously that for the first time user the best thing is to experiment with your lanterns, to find out just what they will do for you in your venue. It's important for the first time designer that if possible you do actually make these experiments and assessments in your venue, for looking at the performance of a lantern in any other location, will probably give you a false impression.

Of course, all of us being individual and original thinkers will mean that we will all want to experiment and try something new or different. Quite right too, but where your experimentation with lighting is concerned, I suggest that anything too radical, like reinventing the old traditional footlight position, or using a total rig of profile lanterns each with a hard focused gobo, is not the sort of thing to spring onto your production team at the first plotting session – well certainly not without some prior warning. If it doesn't work and you have to change it you will be having a late night and probably have to buy all the crew drinks for a week! Experiment by all means, try something new, but try not to let it eat into that precious technical time to the detriment of the production overall.

Plotting – the Lighting Technical

So having got this far with an understanding of what the different lantern types will do for you, being happy about the positions that they are working from to give you the desired angles to light your subjects, made your colour choice and having focused everything, you arrive at the plotting session where your combined efforts will be put together and seen by you (and others) for the first time. Not nervous about this are we?

Don't worry, I think most people are, even seasoned professionals. It's the equivalent of the writer's 'clean sheet of paper' for many a nerve jangling moment. What will happen if people don't like what you produce? Probably worse is what happens if *you* don't like what you've produced. Well, there is something that the beginner can do about that, assuming you have the benefit of a memory lighting control desk.

The plotting session, lighting session, lighting technical, whatever you call it, is where you, your director, stage management and probably most of the production team will gather at the 'production desk'[1] in the auditorium, so that you can present your offerings of lighting. Try to get ahead of the game, it's always a good idea if you and your lighting operator (or perhaps it's just you

---

1 Production Desk: A worktop, average size 2m x1.5m. Most performance spaces will have their own version, which will rest on top of the seating in the auditorium providing a location to spread out your lighting plan layout, various other stage management paperwork, one or more communication headsets and a working light.

Nominally you, the director and the member of stage management who is running the book (calling the show) will be working from this position.

filling both roles) spend a little more of that mythical spare time you have in setting up a few lighting states and committing them to your memory control desk before you all sit down for the real plotting session. A memory control desk with submasters is particularly useful in this process, as it will give you the opportunity to split your lighting into specific sections: you could have four submasters set up to contain (1) all warm colour coverage from stage left (2) all warm cover coverage from stage right and (3) and (4) providing the same but in the cold coverage. Then you could have side lighting, back lighting, cyclorama lighting, etc, all set up on any number of additional submasters. Think of them as your building blocks of light because you can add and mix them together until you achieve the balance you are after, then memorise the mix either onto another submaster or into a regular memory, somewhere in the high number end of your control desk's capacity. This way, when you sit down for the plotting session you should have a little more confidence that what you produce will actually look like you intended. It will also speed up the plotting session as you will be able to bring up multiple combinations of lanterns rather than have to bring up each one in turn. Of course, once you have offered your lighting state built from your submaster selections, you have the opportunity to dip into it at any position (lantern) to individually increase or decrease an intensity level, or deselect or include any lantern of your choice.

Depending upon the mix of people at the production desk helping with the plotting session, you might be receiving comments not only from the director, but also the set and costume designers. Again there is no hard or fast rule of engagement where this is concerned. It would be quite normal, indeed expected, that the director would have a large say in the acceptance of your lighting because it's the director that has responsibility for the overall look and performance of the production. But what of the others? The set designer is obviously very interested in the 'look' of the set and scenery they have produced and it can sometimes be a fraught and long drawn out session if the designer keeps asking you to provide specific lighting coverage just to accentuate a part of the set when all your efforts and available equipment had gone into lighting the performers. Production styles and set designs vary and often it is obvious that the set and scenery can benefit from some specific lighting treatment, while at other times it may seem that the set designer is wanting too much attention paid to their masterpieces to the detriment of the overall lighting, and just when you think you have that little battle under control, the costume designer will suggest that the fabric of one of the principals costumes, "would look a little better if the overall colour wash was a shade darker"!

Of course, for the vast majority of you these considerations won't be relevant, because you won't have the benefit of a set or costume designer, well not in the strict descriptive terms anyway. Your group will have one or more people who build the set, maybe from an existing assembly of scenic flats or cloths and then apply a paint finish, while the performers might wear nondescript street clothes, or be using hired in costumes, in any event without the benefit of a costume designer. So it's probably down to just you, the director and a member of the stage management team to agree on the lighting states.

The stage management involvement in the plotting session is two-fold (two *person* fold) with one sitting at the production desk who is interested in the lighting changes needed and their timing, but who won't usually have much input into the look of the lighting state created except to confirm that the areas covered mirror the actions of the acting company. The second member of the stage management team will probably be 'walking the set'. This will give you and the director a confirmation that the area is covered and a first glimpse of what the set and your lighting actually look like with real people in place.

Talk of Teamwork Again – a Nostalgic View

As you might expect, where you are involved in a team of people that work regularly together – director, designers, stage management – they get to know each other's abilities, likes and dislikes, so much of the talking and planning is just an ongoing working relationship. Without wishing to sound too old, in the days of true repertory theatre the rep company was often described as the place for the acting company to learn their trade. Well, the same thing goes for those working in the technical departments. Sadly there's not much true repertory theatre left these days, because most producing theatres will hire in guest directors and designers. The old format of having a group of the same people producing different productions is rather frowned upon as being repetitive and old fashioned, but it had a glamour and credibility all of its own. Those of you working at the amateur level probably get quite close to that old rep company team spirit, so much of what I'm talking about won't be a surprise to you and those of you working at an education-based level may have a two or three year cycle of people in your team, then just when the individuals become useful, they leave and the teaching and learning process starts all over again.

The Dress Rehearsal

Just a brief but important note about the role of the lighting designer at the dress rehearsal. You might think your work is nearly over, maybe everyone is happy with your lighting, but be a little self-critical without being over picky. You can usually find one or two things that could be improved just a little, maybe a small adjustment in the focus here and there, or changing that piece of wrong colour that has crept in, unnoticed by everyone except you. And perhaps most important, take a wander around the auditorium and look at your lighting and the overall production from different seats, you might be surprised at how it all looks – being different, not necessarily wrong – to the front and centre view from the production desk.

For many people this process won't stop at the dress rehearsal, it may continue into the first night and even throughout the production run. It's amazing what you can learn from watching your end product 'in use', which of course will help you with the next production.

4 THE DESIGN INTO PRACTICE

So let's recap: just where have we got to in the considerations of lighting design?

1) We have talked about the style of lighting, being either 'realistic' or 'surrealistic'.
2) We have considered whether you are providing the design concepts or if you are asked to deliver other people's ideas and requirements.
3) I have tried to promote the use of the lighting coverage, probably in two colours, as a major factor in your design.
4) A distinction has been made between performance lighting for the audience and lighting for film or video.
5) I have made countless references to time and its allocation in your lighting works.
6) The importance of the 'critical focus' and the positions of your lanterns have been shown to be vital in your lighting.

True, there are other things that can't be discounted, but these six areas are probably the most important, and I suggest warrant inclusion in your lighting efforts. They are all things which, even if not tangible hardware, will affect your work. The next step is to get something out of your conceptual ideas and recorded on paper.

Your Rig Plan

I'm probably not telling many of you something you don't already know, but for the novice lighting designer you are going to need to make a plan of your intended equipment (lanterns) and their location in relation to the setting you are working in. I covered this in *Basics – A Beginner's Guide to Stage Lighting* and because of its importance, I include it again here.

The rig plan is often a true scale drawing of the stage area, with the confines of the set drawn on it, the rig of lanterns also being scale representations of your equipment. If scale drawings are not available then a schematic representation can be used. This is fine for smaller events,

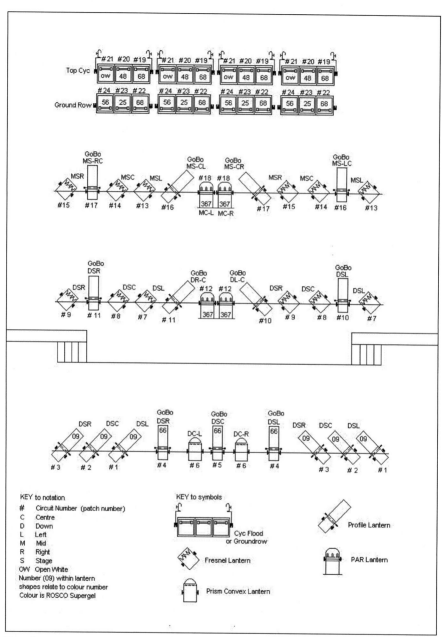

Rig plan.

venues and rigs but where you are working on a large project the scale imaging becomes very helpful and practically essential.

Your rig plan will contain not only the graphic information of set and lantern positions but should also give specific notation on at least three other major factors:

1.The circuit/dimmer number (represented by #or circled) associated with each lantern:#4

2.The approximate focus position: DSL (down stage left).

3.The colour, even if no colour, used in the lantern:122 usually circled, no colour is normally shown as o/w (open white).

The circuit number #4 is normally placed behind the lantern, the colour normally placed within the representation of the lantern shape and the focus position normally placed in front of the lantern.

The rig plan will contain various other notes on the use of barndoors, iris, gobo and shutters, indeed anything that is relevant to the focus operation and depending upon the size of the rig involved it can become a rather complex document. I suggest that however simple your rig plan is, it's not likely to fit on a sheet of A4!

If you have a tried and tested format for producing a rig plan then none of this will be new to you. If you are trying this for the first time you may benefit from the purchase of a lantern stencil, which will provide you with the various graphics you are likely to need in representing your lanterns.

Your rig plan has a number of functions – apart from checking your lantern coverage on a white surface! In the professional sense the designer will send the rig plan to the venue so that other people can put the equipment in place prior to the arrival of the designer (don't laugh too much, this really is how it happens in the professional theatre).The information, graphic, numeric and notation, really does have to get written down somewhere. It's not a good idea for the whole thing to stay only within the head of the designer. Finally, when you come to the plotting session you will need to know circuit numbers etc, so the plan becomes quite a vital part of your lighting design.

Your design obviously starts off in your head, but the 'rig plan' is about as close as you get to writing it down. You may make notes while sitting in on rehearsals, and these might be general observations relating to the blocking of the acting company, or be specific to a particular piece of action that requires a lighting change or effect. You might be the type that makes copious notes, or be happy to just watch the rehearsal, making hardly any notes at all. You might take the opportunity during rehearsals to talk with the director and stage management team about specific lighting requirements and changes (lighting cues). In the most part this will be dependent upon the director and whether he or she wants to spend time talking technical issues. But the notes you take don't often find their way onto your rig plan, well not in quite the same way as you noted them in the rehearsal.

The rig plan is really a technical hardware schedule and for some it's a way of turning your mind's eye intentions into the hardware needed to make it happen in the real world. If you think about a requirement for your area coverage, you will be drawing and positioning lanterns on your rig plan to fulfil just that function, likewise for every other element of lighting you intend to use.

Some will perhaps argue, saying that they don't need to see it on paper to know that it will work. I can't disagree, for it's true that what I might imagine as a lighting condition can't be represented by lines and images on a sheet of paper. The actual image that I have in mind will stay with me until I see it turned into reality on stage. But for the beginner, the act of getting it down on paper should help – anyway the rig plan isn't necessarily intended to be the interpretation of your mind's eye view, only the hardware needed to let everyone see what equipment you intend to use to create your ideas.

You might think there's a lot more to come; surely there must be more to it than your ideas and a rig plan? Well yes there is, but the majority of it really is in the conception and planning and a lot of this will rely on your understanding of what the equipment will do, coupled with your ability, through time, budget and the physical locations available to rig your lanterns.

What this leads you to is the fact that unless you have this level of understanding regarding the equipment and its positioning, you can't really expect to offer any sort of meaningful lighting design. Now I don't want to complicate things too much, but that last statement isn't actually correct. Remember my comments almost at the beginning about whether it was your design or someone else's? Well chances are that if it's someone else's then that someone probably has the ideas of what it should look like, but very little knowledge or understanding about the ability of the equipment.

So where is all this taking us in my efforts to help you with a lighting design process? Simply to help you identify just where you are in the process needed to produce lighting for your event. You would probably expect that coming from someone who has been a paid professional lighting designer my vote would always be for the design to come from someone who had the complete level of information, not just the conceptual view. This brings us full circle in the design process and a return to you seeking information from others during the planning of your production. The final part of this process, indeed it's often separated by many days or weeks, is when you sit down at the plotting session and lighting technical and offer your interpretation of that original information gathered.

This whole issue of concepts and the knowledge needed to turn those concepts into reality is perhaps the one reason why there is sometimes a question mark about the role of the lighting designer, being within or outside of the artistic team, because as I have made reference to before, many would see the requirement as simply rigging and operation. How do you feel about that? Well, whatever your view, you had better make sure that your production team is aware of it, because it will help everybody understand their roles and responsibilities in the mounting of your production.

Surprises!

Within the lighting you create for your production, you will sometimes find that you can create a lighting condition or lighting effect that you hadn't planned or intended. It might be the effect of a colour you have used that really brings out a particular colour within the set or costumes, it could be just one individual lantern and its critical focus that lights a performer or a feature of the set in a particular way, or a combination of lanterns the light outputs of which create multi-coloured shadow images. Whatever these special things are, rejoice, they are the bonus and the unplanned benefits that you can get from your design. Of course if you are smart, you will be able to hide your surprise, joy, even incredulity and claim that you planned it that way all along! It's true to say that the more lanterns you use in your design, the more likely you are to see things like this, but it's equally true to say, that even a small quantity of equipment can throw up some pleasant surprises.

There is of course the downside surprise, where the coverage or effect you had planned to produce simply doesn't work, or at least does not come up to the expectations of your concept. In these cases you probably have some work to do, but don't despair, think positively. At least you will have allocated some lanterns and dimmer channels to create the desired lighting, so if you're lucky you probably just need to tweak the focus a little. If you're not so lucky you might have to re-rig your lanterns into different locations. If you find out this sort of thing at the plotting session, you need to throw yourself on the mercy of the director with the promise that you will "get it all sorted after the plotting session". If it's a relatively simple problem, like a coverage that doesn't quite do the job, or a particular special lantern focused for a one-off effect, then you will probably get away with fixing it at a later time, but if it's a lighting state or effect that's really vital to the whole event, then you just might need to stop the session and get it sorted there and then. That's another good reason for using my advice. To spend a little time before the actual plotting session in which to 'play' with your lighting, and creating a few states, and will often mean there are no unpleasant surprises lying in wait for you.

Homework

After the completion of the plotting session and lighting technical it's normal for the control desk operator to spend some time tidying up the nuts and bolts of the lighting operation job, and this can involve a number of different tasks. With the smaller old manual preset type control desks, there will be a requirement for the preset sheets to be written up clearly and checks made with stage management to ensure there is enough time between lighting cues in which to achieve the preset changes needed. In memory control desk operation, it may have been that the memories and lighting states held within submasters used to achieve the lighting at the plotting session were non-consecutive. But for easy use in operation, it is preferable that they appear as a consecutive string of memory numbers. This usually means that the control desk is able to run in sequence mode i.e. starting at memory No1 and progressing in sequence number order right through the show. This way there is less actual button pressing for the operator to do (which by default means a lower error factor) leaving more time to concentrate on the actual cue operation and manual timing where needed. So the operator will effectively be editing the lighting states, but only in the order of entry in memory numbers, not their content.

All this of course is not normally of any consequence to you and the lighting design process, except that a conscientious control desk operator who understands the requirements of the task and who spends time with things such as this tidy up process is likely to produce an operational performance that can only help to enhance your lighting design.

External Influences

Just as the control desk operator can help to present your lighting as you intended, there are others within the technical team and outside it that can affect things. The first and most obvious cause for concern are the mechanics involved in getting instructions for the lighting changes to your control desk operator.

This function carries a number of descriptive names within the technical theatre industry: 'cueing' or 'calling the show' probably being the most common, but whatever name you give it, it's the action of a member of your stage management team who does the job. It's another topic that I covered in *Basics – A Beginners Guide to Stage Lighting* and again because of its importance I include it here.

> *There are two important points to note. I know that many amateur companies and lots of others who simply don't know any better will say that "our lighting people take all their cues themselves from reading their own copy of the script".*
>
> *Well, not in my world they don't. It's just not possible to read text, watch the stage and work the control desk all at the same time with any degree of success, even in a slow moving two handed play, let alone a fast moving musical. No, it all comes down to the stage manager, for it's this person's job to bring together all the technical departments so that they are given all the information they need to do the relevant technical job at the right time.*
>
> *The second critical point, which also involves the stage manager, is the language used – not the profanities, but the actual words and their order when used in talking to the technical departments. Most technical theatre in performance uses a communications system whereby each operator and the stage manager wears a headset (earphones) with a microphone so that everybody can give and receive information. Those using such a system for the first time should be (must be!) discouraged from idle chatter. The 'comms' network is not in place to discuss the football results, organise the after show party or any topic other than the technical job in hand. And it's at this point that the order of words and the language used is vitally important.*
>
> *Stage Manager: "Stand By Electrics (LX) cue 47".*
>
> *Lighting Control: "LX cue 47 standing by".*
>
> *The stage manager will have agreed the length of the stand by period beforehand with all technical operators.*
>
> *Stage Manager: "LX cue 47 GO".*
>
> *Lighting Control will action the cue on the command word GO. It all looks and sounds very simple – and it is – but just put yourself in the position of the*

stage manager who has to give technical cues to all departments: lighting, sound, off stage effects, flys, followspots and any number of others as well as, in addition to calling the acting company from the dressing rooms, keeping times of the performance, and following the script or score. And he could be prompting the acting company if needed. If you have a good stage manager do all you can to keep him or her, for this person will help make your show a success. A bad one who panics at the slightest hint of a problem, however, can ruin your technical efforts and should be encouraged to find an alternative way of spending their evening.

The point about language and order of words is that the command word GO must be the last word given, so that the control operator, already on standby, is given all of the information again just prior to the action. LX lets the operator know this is for them and no other technical department. Cue 47 gives again the precise nature of the cue to be performed, GO being the exact moment that the change is made or started. Don't forget that the technical department put on standby should acknowledge this to the stage manager as follows: "LX standing by cue 47".

But why is this so relevant? Because the system of cueing must be geared to the most needful situation, such as when a lighting cue, with instant effect, must be performed at a precise moment in the action, for instance when an actor switches on a table lamp or light switch. Yes, I know that in the main this type of cue is taken as a visual cue by the lighting operator, but there will come a time when the operator must rely on the stage manager to give the cue in exactly the right place, so the method of giving the cue must be correct and the same every time.

So having made sure that your technical team are going to use the correct method of cueing, what else could affect your lighting? Well quite a few things, some coming under the heading of "life's battle with inanimate objects" and some unfortunate actions with a human element attached.

Taking the Murphy's law things first, the most obvious is blown lamps, and you might think there's not much you can do about that. Not quite true. Remember my scenario of the sales conference, with the simple lighting of someone standing at a lectern? Now take on board my promptings about lighting your performer from two front positions, and you will imagine that your presenter at the lectern will indeed be lit by two lanterns (more if you have managed to provide a little back light). If you have these lanterns connected to the same dimmer circuit and one should suffer a lamp failure, you will in fact lose both lanterns because the fuse will blow or circuit breaker trip out.

End result, no front light on your presenter – embarrassing. Now if you had the presence of mind to plan for an attack of Murphy's law, you might have made sure that the two lanterns were on separate dimmer channels, so if you lost one lantern, at least your presenter would not be left completely in the dark! This thought and planning process really should be in your thinking for every critical area of the lighting coverage.

I know that for the vast majority of users the concept of one lantern to one dimmer is simply just not possible, but where it's critical to the event, that's how you should plan and think. This is perhaps taking us into the realms of advanced lighting works and away from the *basic* principles of this book but let's face it, it's not a complicated thought process.

Of course, having individual dimmers won't help if the lamp failure happens to be in the one lantern you need for a particular coverage, but there are two things that can help you here: the first is in your planning, and again harping back to my continued references to covering areas with more than one lantern. I know that if it was a 'special' lantern that failed and you could only cover the specific area with a general coverage lantern, the use of the latter is not likely to provide the same lighting condition that you intended, but what's preferable - general light on the area or no light at all? The second part of this lies within the speed and efficiency of the control desk operator. Firstly they have to be familiar with the focus of all of the lanterns and secondly they need to have the technical ability to add or substitute a new lantern (dimmer channel) into the lighting state – live, on the run – during the action of the normal lighting cues; this of course being a smooth and seamless happening. It's when things like this happen that you start to realise just how skilled you need to be as a lighting control desk operator, for while the modern computer technology will help in these things, the skill is with the operator, for one false button press while attempting this sort of action could plunge the whole show into darkness or some other irrelevant lighting state.

Having praised the potential skill of your control desk operator, there is of course the other side of the coin: the operator who has little or no skill, ability, attention to detail, no sense of timing, no feel for the task in hand, behaves like an automaton, or has implicit faith in the power of the computer, thinking that when you press the button it will be perfect every time! I think you get the idea.

Then there are the other human factors which will manifest themselves in many different ways: there are the flies or stage crew who have an uncanny knack of unfocusing one or more of your lanterns with the none-too-careful use of a piece of scenery or flown cloth and of course the acting company who, despite painstaking hours in rehearsal, will insist on standing in the wrong place, thus not being able to enjoy the benefit of the lighting you put in place for them. But I have saved the most relevant and the most dangerous of all till last: the followspot operator.

This is yet another of those all or nothing situations, for a good followspot operator will add their talent to the event, providing that smooth seamless thing that I keep talking about, and just like your lighting for lots of applications, it won't be noticed, commented upon or even thanked.

But if you get a bad one, whose sole intent is to make sure that everyone sees the followspot because of its jerky actions, its inability to simply follow the artist, to come on half way up the proscenium arch and then hunt around in the darkness to find the artist, to flick colours in and out like some demented disco fitting – I could go on, but the memories are almost too painful. When trying to make the case for proper followspot operation when dealing with a rookie operator, I usually use the following analogy.

If I had decided to use different shades of green colour in every lantern in my lighting rig, the audience would think it very odd. They may question my design concept, even my sanity, but they wouldn't necessarily think of it as wrong. Odd maybe, but not wrong. Now take the followspot covering the artist standing front and centre, full body coverage in white light; the artist now moves a pace left or right and the followspot doesn't move with him (assuming it's not a planned joke). Everyone in the audience instantly sees that the followspot operator has made a mistake!

That's the basic thing about followspots – they're big bright chunks of light, which are meant to be seen, so when you make a mistake with one, it's instantly visible to all. You can probably tell that I have a bit of a passion about followspots. Like so many before and after me, it's where I started in the theatre world and it really hurts to see poor followspot operation. Perhaps I should write *Basics – a Beginner's Guide to Followspot Operation* and really get it off my chest!

Strangely, the lighting designer doesn't always have much input to the followspots in a production, unless they make it their business to do so, which I think they always should; for as I have described, the actions of the followspot can have an impact – for better or for worse – on the lighting that you are tasked to provide. As the lighting designer, I would want to set the parameters as to how the followspots look and work, i.e. are they working with a hard or soft edge? Do they fade in and out with the action of a dowser shutter or do they iris-down to blackout? I would want to make the choice of colours used and, if inexperienced, make sure the operators have at least some time to practice with them. Incidentally, speaking as a time-served followspot operator, I do have one comment to make on the hardware. They (and the operators) don't need 'sights'. This modern gimmick has become the norm and I find it rather insulting, since the operator should be able to regard the aim point of the followspot as an extension of their arms or eye line, developing a high degree of accuracy even in blackout conditions.

Finally, and as a glimpse into the not too distant future, my vision of the followspot in its ultimate and fully developed form, will be a comfortable armchair at the rear of the auditorium where the operator will sit wearing a 'head up infrared display' and using fingertip controls for movement on the extended right or left armrest, the other having iris, blackout and colour selection controls. The actual lantern itself, whatever the light source and capacity, will be motor servo controlled and probably nowhere near the operator in the comfy chair. A little far-fetched? Just wait and see.

5 CONCLUSIONS

Having said at the outset that it's difficult to provide the definitive "how to do lighting design", mainly because of all of the variables involved, I have goaded myself into writing down quite a few things that I feel are really relevant to the lighting design process. So just to annoy those of you who have read this far (because if you had known you could have saved the time and turned to this page when you picked up the book) let me recap on what I regard as the most relevant points.

- There are two major conceptual considerations to be made about your lighting:
  1) Is it to be a seamless part of the overall event? or
  2) Is it to be effective in its own right, adding an important facet to the overall end product?
- In being a designer you are virtually hanging a big sign round your neck that says "artist", or at least a person who has to deliver an end product allied to an artistic interpretation.
- If you are asked to design the lighting for a theatrical production, how much of a free hand do you actually have? Are you being asked (probably by the director or producer) to provide *your* interpretation for the lighting or are you following the ideas and interpretations of others? In short, you aren't really designing anything at all: your role will be to rig, focus and operate.
- Whichever method your design is based upon – your own interpretation or someone else's - the conceptual starting point for the design will probably need input from a few other people, at least in gathering information about the style of the piece to be lit.
- There is of course a classification of 'lighting design' which really puts all of the decision making onto you, without the help or guidance from a production team. It may be that you are tasked to light a non-theatrical event or presentation.
- I made reference to lighting for performance needing to be accentuated. Now even for the realistic type of lighting you are going to produce a lighting condition, which by the nature of being in

a performance space, is not exactly realistic but it needs to follow the ideas and have an end product of a realistic condition.

- Within your specific venue you probably have an existing assembly of lanterns, or at least the positions from which to suspend and rig lanterns. If you are new to this task and if indeed this is to be your first attempt at lighting design, then you really are going to need some information on just what the lanterns can and cannot do for you. They are the tools of your trade, they are the start and almost the end of your lighting efforts.

- I have made several references to time, and this factor, even above your budget, is likely to be the deciding factor in what your design concept can actually produce.

- The real problem is that for those whose technology has stood still, their expectations probably have not, and the consequence of this is that some of you will be expected to produce the 21st century end product, but only be able to use 20th century tools. You don't need to be a genius to realise that this isn't likely to work and of course there's no magic answer to it, except money and time.

- Lanterns, types and sizes, and where to use them. Yes size and capacity does matter. Lanterns too small and thus under-powered for the size of the venue simply won't be able to provide the light intensity needed to do the job. Likewise, over-sized lanterns are a waste since you will hardly ever use them to their full capacity and they will look out of place hanging in a smaller venue.

- The three-area two-colour coverage.
    1) Concentrate on an even area coverage, even if only in one colour, and cover each area from two positions, providing a front lit coverage to your audience.
    2) If you can identify the specific requirement, you may be able to cover the area warm form one side and cold from the other. Just remember that's what you will have for every lighting state, but if it works for you, then fine.
    3) Consider those angles, too shallow or too steep and you are creating problems for yourself.

- Remember, a group of lanterns focused onto individual areas of the performance stage for a specific effect may not be able to provide an even overall coverage of light, but the focus of lanterns into an even overall coverage will probably be able to provide the individual area's coverage.

- I have to go over some old ground here, in what I call 'The Critical Focus' and if there was ever one golden rule in lighting design, it would be this. *"Get the focus right, because lanterns focused in the wrong place simply can't do the job"*. We'll forgo but not forget the part about getting the lanterns in the right position. I'll come back to this, but what I'm talking about here is the actual mechanical hands-on focusing of the lantern.

- Don't light the floor and forget the actors! In the typical example of lighting the floor but not the actor, you can also see the relevance of the positioning of lanterns *in the right place*. As I said, it's a 50/50 thing. Yes, the critical focus has to be correct, but then so does the position of the lantern. I know I'm repeating myself, but I can't stress enough just how important and critical this will be to your lighting efforts.

- Even with the correct equipment, the focus session will take a lot more of that precious time than you expect, even where you are working in a venue with high level walkways behind each lighting bar, it's still not a speedy operation. Obviously the overall size of the event and the numbers of lanterns involved will be a major factor, but as a final note on the focus procedure, don't rush it, take the time you need to get it right.

- So having got this far with an understanding of what the different lantern types will do for you, being happy about the positions that they are working from to give you the desired angles to light your subjects, made your colour choice and focused everything, you arrive at the plotting session where your combined efforts will be put together and seen by you (and others) for the first time. Not nervous about this are we?

- The rig plan is really a technical hardware schedule and for some it's a way of turning your mind's eye intentions into the hardware needed to make it happen in the real world.

- Just as the control desk operator can help to present your lighting as you intended, there are others within the technical team and outside it, who can affect things.

Resumé over, these buzz word phrases and bullet points are what it all comes down to. They are those things which need your attention and consideration. You do need to put the flesh back onto the bones of each heading as to miss one out or disregard it as 'not important' will probably be to the detriment of all of your efforts.

It might be difficult for you at the outset of your work in lighting design, but keep at it. Experience will bring with it the strength for you to have courage in your design convictions. Like many of us, you will come to realise the wonderful creative part of working with light on the clean canvas of a performance stage, suddenly to realise that many have created something similar before. There's not much that hasn't been tried and tested, but that's not the real point, it's the performance that's relevant. Your lighting creativity will be extinguished with the last fade to blackout, put back into your memory where it came from, stored away and left to ferment until you bring it out again, with a little more substance, a little more finesse, hopefully never to be just a regurgitated repeat.

Enjoy it, remember as Eric Morecambe said: "We'll have the lighting on". I hope that in some small way these few pages may have helped you in your efforts.

GLOSSARY

This list is by no means comprehensive; it is intended only to give a quick reference to those names and phrases that cause most confusion to the beginner.

#	A symbol used to denote the dimmer circuit number (#4) on a rig plan.
Axial Lamp	A range of new tungsten halogen lamps in which the filament of the lamp is designed to operate in an almost horizontal plane with the lamp cap above the level of the filament.
Aspheric Lens	A new lens type used in Profile lanterns where the density/thickness of the lens is reduced producing a lighter/thinner lens able to transmit more light.
Blocking	The instructions by the director (choreographer) in positioning the acting company in a particular position on stage, being noted down by stage management.
Box Set	A stage set, normally a room interior, made up of scenery flats.
Cinemoid	Discontinued range of colour filter.
Colour Temperature	The light output of a lamp, referenced to the Kelvin temperature scale.
Coverage	Multiple lanterns combining together to cover a larger area than can be achieved with a single lantern, sometimes called a 'wash' or 'colour wash' of light.
Cueing	The instructions given by stage management to command technical departments, lighting, sound, etc, to action a change, 'giving a cue'.
Dichroic Reflector	The glass reflector within a modern lantern.
Diffusion Filter	An opaque filter material used on its own or combined with other colour filters, to "diffuse" the light output of a lantern.
Dress Rehearsal	Nominally the last rehearsal before a production opens to the public.

Effect Lighting   Lighting where the lighting itself is visible, i,e, moving cloud images, gobo projection, water wave ripples, etc.

Effective Lighting
Lighting where the lighting condition created adds to the overall effect of the production.

End Stage   Sometimes referred to as 'proscenium arch' stage presentation, where the seated audience views the event taking place upon a stage at one end of a large room or space.

Flat Field   The setting within a profile lantern enabling the light to fill the complete image to a uniform intensity.

Flood (lantern)   One of five lantern types, a flood having no lens, but simply a means of suspension, pan and tilt.

Focusing   The act of setting a lantern to produce its light output in a precise or particular way.

Follow Spot   A large profile lantern requiring manual operation.

Fresnel   One of five lanterns types, The Fresnel taking its name from the inventor of the lens. The lantern produces a variable light output with a diffused/soft edge to the light beam.

Gobo   A small metal (sometimes glass) disc used within a profile lantern, etched with a pattern or design, turning the profile lantern into an image projector.

Hard Focus   The ability of a profile lantern to produce a clear sharp 'hard' edge to the light output.

Lee Filters   A major manufacturer of colour filter.

Masking Shutter   One of usually four masking shutter blades found within a profile lantern, to control the light path by masking portions of its output.

Memory Control Desk
A lighting control desk containing a function to memorise/record information (lighting states) and reproduce/replay this information, under control of an operator.

Pastel Colours   Lighter shades of colour filter.

PAR One of five lanterns types, the PAR (Parabolic Aluminised Reflector) a high intensity, low cost lantern, specially useful for where deep saturated colours are required.

Peak Field Adjustment
The setting within a profile lantern enabling the light to be concentrated at the centre of the image, creating a centre 'hot spot'.

Plotting The action of setting lighting states and the notation or actions of memorising them for use in the performance.

Preset Desk Old style lighting control desk, consisting of two duplicate sets of faders, corresponding to the numbers of dimmers to be controlled, each set of faders having a master fader, permitting the action of 'presetting' a lighting state.

Prism Convex One of five lanterns types, the prism convex also known as the 'PC', is similar to the Fresnel but uses a different lens, giving a slightly more defined edge to the light beam.

Production Desk A worktop, which will rest on top of the seating in the auditorium, providing a location for the lighting designer, stage management and director to work from.

Profile Lantern One of five lanterns types, the profile lantern will contain one or more plain convex lenses and produce a light output with a hard defined edge – the only lantern that can use a gobo.

Realistic (lighting)
Lighting which mimics real life conditions, where the lighting is not intended to be noticed for its own sake, but should blend into the overall appearance of the production.

Rigging The act of putting equipment (lanterns) in place, being both a mechanical and electrical process.

Rig Plan A paper plan (usually to scale) showing the confines of the set and stage area and all the lighting equipment (lanterns) used to light the production.

Rosco A major manufacturer of colour filter, gobos and scenic materials.

Saturated Colours
Deep colour filter.

Saturation Rig Lighting rig comprising many hundreds of lanterns.

Standard Rig and Focus

A standard configuration of lanterns and their focus, adopted in venues where multiple use and fast turn around are the norm.

Submasters
A facility found within most memory lighting control desks, where an individual fader (submaster) can have multiple dimmer channels selected under its control.

Surrealistic (lighting)

Lighting which does not mimic any realistic condition, where the lighting is intended to be noticed for the effect it creates.

Tallescope
Industry standard piece of equipment (ladder) used as means of access to rig and focus equipment above a performance stage space.

Technical Rehearsal

A rehearsal of technical facilities, set, properties, lighting, sound, technical crew, etc. where no acting or performing company is involved.

Tungsten Halogen

A lamp having a tungsten filament and a halogen gas infill.

Walking the Set/Stage

The actions undertaken by a member of the stage management team, to 'walk the stage' so that the lighting can be seen to have covered the correct areas, this happening during the plotting session.

ENTERTAINMENT TECHNOLOGY PRESS

FREE SUBSCRIPTION SERVICE

Keeping Up To Date with

Basics – A Beginner's Guide to Lighting Design

Entertainment Technology titles are continually up-dated, and all major changes and additions are listed in date order in the relevant dedicated area of the publisher's website. Simply go to the front page of www.etnow.com and click on the BOOKS button. From there you can locate the title and be connected through to the latest information and services related to the publication.

The author of the title welcomes comments and suggestions about the book and can be contacted by email at:
basics@etnow.com

Titles Published by Entertainment Technology Press

ABC of Theatre Jargon *Francis Reid* **£9.95** ISBN 1904031099
This glossary of theatrical terminology explains the common words and phrases that are
used in normal conversation between actors, directors, designers, technicians and managers.

Aluminium Structures in the Entertainment Industry *Peter Hind* **£24.95**
ISBN 1904031064
Aluminium Structures in the Entertainment Industry aims to educate the reader in all aspects
of the design and safe usage of temporary and permanent aluminium structures specific to
the entertainment industry – such as roof structures, PA towers, temporary staging, etc.

AutoCAD – A Handbook for Theatre Users *David Ripley* **£24.95** ISBN 1904031315
From 'Setting Up' to 'Drawing in Three Dimensions' via 'Drawings Within Drawings', this
compact and fully illustrated guide to AutoCAD covers everything from the basics to full colour
rendering and remote plotting.

Basics – A Beginner's Guide to Lighting Design *Peter Coleman* **£9.95** ISBN 1904031412
The fourth in the author's 'Basics' series, this title covers the subject area in four main
sections: The Concept, Practical Matters, Related Issues and The Design Into Practice. In an
area that is difficult to be difinitive, there are several things that cross all the boundaries of
all lighting design and it's these areas that the author seeks to help with.

Basics – A Beginner's Guide to Special Effects *Peter Coleman* **£9.95** ISBN 1904031331
This title introduces newcomers to the world of special effects. It describes all types
of special effects including pyrotechnic, smoke and lighting effects, projections, noise
machines, etc. It places emphasis on the safe storage, handling and use of pyrotechnics.

Basics – A Beginner's Guide to Stage Lighting *Peter Coleman* **£9.95** ISBN 190403120X
This title does what it says: it introduces newcomers to the world of stage lighting. It will
not teach the reader the art of lighting design, but will teach beginners much about the 'nuts
and bolts' of stage lighting.

Basics – A Beginner's Guide to Stage Sound *Peter Coleman* **£9.95** ISBN 1904031277
This title does what it says: it introduces newcomers to the world of stage sound. It will not
teach the reader the art of sound design, but will teach beginners much about the background
to sound reproduction in a theatrical environment.

Building Better Theaters *Michael Mell* **£16.95** 1904031404
A title within our Consultancy Series, this book describes the process of designing a theater,
from the initial decision to build through to opening night. Mr. Mell's book provides a
step-by-step guide to the design and construction of performing arts facilities. Chapters
discuss: assembling your team, selecting an architect, different construction methods, the
architectural design process, construction of the theater, theatrical systems and equipment,
the stage, backstage, the auditorium, ADA requirements and the lobby. Each chapter
clearly describes what to expect and how to avoid surprises. It is a must-read for architects,
planners, performing arts groups, educators and anyone who may be considering building or
renovating a theater.

A Comparative Study of Crowd Behaviour at Two Major Music Events
Chris Kemp, Iain Hill, Mick Upton **£7.95** ISBN 1904031250
A compilation of the findings of reports made at two major live music concerts, and in particular crowd behaviour, which is followed from ingress to egress.

Copenhagen Opera House *Richard Brett and John Offord* **£32.00** ISBN 1904031420
Completed in a little over three years, the Copenhagen Opera House opened with a royal gala performance on 15th January 2005. Built on a spacious brown-field site, the building is a landmark venue and this book provides the complete technical background story to an opera house set to become a benchmark for future design and planning. Sixteen chapters by relevant experts involved with the project cover everything from the planning of the auditorium and studio stage, the stage engineering, stage lighting and control and architectural lighting through to acoustic design and sound technology plus technical summaries.

Electrical Safety for Live Events *Marco van Beek* **£16.95** ISBN 1904031285
This title covers electrical safety regulations and good pracitise pertinent to the entertainment industries and includes some basic electrical theory as well as clarifying the "do's and don't's" of working with electricity.

The Exeter Theatre Fire *David Anderson* **£24.95** ISBN 1904031137
This title is a fascinating insight into the events that led up to the disaster at the Theatre Royal, Exeter, on the night of September 5th 1887. The book details what went wrong, and the lessons that were learned from the event.

Fading Light – A Year in Retirement *Francis Reid* **£14.95** ISBN 1904031358
Francis Reid, the lighting industry's favourite author, describes a full year in retirement. "Old age is much more fun than I expected," he says. Fading Light describes visits and experiences to the author's favourite theatres and opera houses, places of relaxation and re-visits to scholarly intitutions.

Focus on Lighting Technology *Richard Cadena* **£17.95** ISBN 1904031145
This concise work unravels the mechanics behind modern performance lighting and appeals to designers and technicians alike. Packed with clear, easy-to-read diagrams, the book provides excellent explanations behind the technology of performance lighting.

Health and Safety Aspects in the Live Music Industry *Chris Kemp, Iain Hill* **£30.00** ISBN 1904031226
This title includes chapters on various safety aspects of live event production and is written by specialists in their particular areas of expertise.

Health and Safety Management in the Live Music and Events Industry *Chris Hannam* **£25.95** ISBN 1904031307
This title covers the health and safety regulations and their application regarding all aspects of staging live entertainment events, and is an invaluable manual for production managers and event organisers.

Hearing the Light – 50 Years Backstage *Francis Reid* **£24.95** ISBN 1904031188
This highly enjoyable memoir delves deeply into the theatricality of the industry. The author's almost fanatical interest in opera, his formative period as lighting designer at Glyndebourne and his experiences as a theatre administrator, writer and teacher make for a broad and unique background.

An Introduction to Rigging in the Entertainment Industry *Chris Higgs* **£24.95**
ISBN 1904031129
This book is a practical guide to rigging techniques and practices and also thoroughly covers
safety issues and discusses the implications of working within recommended guidelines and
regulations.

Let There be Light – Entertainment Lighting Software Pioneers in Interview
Robert Bell **£32.00** ISBN 1904031242
Robert Bell interviews a distinguished group of software engineers working on
entertainment lighting ideas and products.

Lighting for Roméo and Juliette *John Offord* **£26.95** ISBN 1904031161
John Offord describes the making of the Vienna State Opera production from the lighting
designer's viewpoint – from the point where director Jürgen Flimm made his decision not to
use scenery or sets and simply employ the expertise of LD Patrick Woodroffe.

Lighting Systems for TV Studios *Nick Mobsby* **£45.00** ISBN 1904031005
Lighting Systems for TV Studios, now in its second edition, is the first book specifically
written on the subject and has become the 'standard' resource work for studio planning
and design covering the key elements of system design, luminaires, dimming, control,
data networks and suspension systems as well as detailing the infrastructure items such as
cyclorama, electrical and ventilation. Sensibly TV lighting principles are explained and
some history on TV broadcasting, camera technology and the equipment is provided to
help set the scene! The second edition includes applications for sine wave and distributed
dimming, moving lights, Ethernet and new cool lamp technology.

Lighting Techniques for Theatre-in-the-Round *Jackie Staines* **£24.95**
ISBN 1904031013
Lighting Techniques for Theatre-in-the-Round is a unique reference source for those
working on lighting design for theatre-in-the-round for the first time. It is the first title to
be published specifically on the subject, it also provides some anecdotes and ideas for more
challenging shows, and attempts to blow away some of the myths surrounding lighting in
this format.

Lighting the Stage *Francis Reid* **£14.95** ISBN 1904031080
Lighting the Stage discusses the human relationships involved in lighting design – both
between people, and between these people and technology. The book is written from a
highly personal viewpoint and its 'thinking aloud' approach is one that Francis Reid has
used in his writings over the past 30 years.

Model National Standard Conditions *ABTT/DSA/LGLA* **£20.00** ISBN 1904031110
These *Model National Standard Conditions* covers operational matters and complement *The
Technical Standards for Places of Entertainment*, which describes the physical requirements
for building and maintaining entertainment premises.

Mr Phipps' Theatre *Mark Jones, John Pick* **£17.95** ISBN: 1904031382
Mark Jones and John Pick describe "The Sensational Story of Eastbourne's Royal
Hippodrome" – formerly Eastbourne Theatre Royal. An intriguing narrative, the book sets
the story against a unique social history of the town. Peter Longman, former director of The
Theatres Trust, provides the Foreword.

Pages From Stages *Anthony Field* **£17.95** ISBN 1904031269
Anthony Field explores the changing style of theatres including interior design, exterior design, ticket and seat prices, and levels of service, while questioning whether the theatre still exists as a place of entertainment for regular theatre-goers.

Practical Dimming *Nick Mobsby* **£TBC** ISBN 19040313447
This important and easy to read title covers the history of electrical and electronic dimming, how dimmers work, current dimmer types from around the world, planning of a dimming system, looking at new sine wave dimming technology and distributed dimming. Integration of dimming into different performance venues as well as the necessary supporting electrical systems are fully detailed. Significant levels of information are provided on the many different forms and costs of potential solutions as well as how to plan specific solutions. Architectural dimming for the likes of hotels, museums and shopping centres are included. Practical Dimming is a companion book to Practical DMX and is designed for all involved in the use, operation and design of dimming systems.

Practical DMX *Nick Mobsby* **£16.95** ISBN 19040313668
In this highly topical and important title the author details the principles of DMX, how to plan a network, how to choose equipment and cables, with data on products from around the world, and how to install DMX networks for shows and on a permanently installed basis. The easy style of the book and the helpful fault finding tips, together with a review of different DMX testing devices provide an ideal companion for all lighting technicians and system designers. An introduction to Ethernet and Canbus networks are provided as well tips on analogue networks and protocol conversion.

Practical Guide to Health and Safety in the Entertainment Industry
Marco van Beek **£14.95** ISBN 1904031048
This book is designed to provide a practical approach to Health and Safety within the Live Entertainment and Event industry. It gives industry-pertinent examples, and seeks to break down the myths surrounding Health and Safety.

Production Management *Joe Aveline* **£17.95** ISBN 1904031102
Joe Aveline's book is an in-depth guide to the role of the Production Manager, and includes real-life practical examples and 'Aveline's Fables' – anecdotes of his experiences with real messages behind them.

Rigging for Entertainment: Regulations and Practice *Chris Higgs* **£19.95**
ISBN 1904031218
Continuing where he left off with his highly successful *An Introduction to Rigging in the Entertainment Industry*, Chris Higgs' second title covers the regulations and use of equipment in greater detail.

Rock Solid Ethernet *Wayne Howell* **£24.95** ISBN 1904031293
Although aimed specifically at specifiers, installers and users of entertainment industry systems, this book will give the reader a thorough grounding in all aspects of computer networks, whatever industry they may work in. The inclusion of historical and technical 'sidebars' make for an enjoyable as well as informative read.

Sixty Years of Light Work *Fred Bentham* **£26.95** ISBN 1904031072
This title is an autobiography of one of the great names behind the development of modern stage lighting equipment and techniques.

Sound for the Stage *Patrick Finelli* **£24.95** ISBN 1904031153
Patrick Finelli's thorough manual covering all aspects of live and recorded sound for
performance is a complete training course for anyone interested in working in the field of
stage sound, and is a must for any student of sound.

**Stage Lighting Design in Britain: The Emergence of the Lighting Designer,
1881-1950** *Nigel Morgan* **£17.95** ISBN 190403134X
This book sets out to ascertain the main course of events and the controlling factors that
determined the emergence of the theatre lighting designer in Britain, starting with the
introduction of incandescent electric light to the stage, and ending at the time of the first
public lighting design credits around 1950. The book explores the practitioners, equipment,
installations and techniques of lighting design.

Stage Lighting for Theatre Designers *Nigel Morgan* **£17.95** ISBN 1904031196
This is an updated second edition of Nigel Morgan's popular book for students of theatre
design – outlining all the techniques of stage lighting design.

Technical Marketing Techniques *David Brooks, Andy Collier, Steve Norman* **£24.95** ISBN
190403103X
Technical Marketing is a novel concept, recently defined and elaborated by the authors of
this book, with business-to-business companies competing in fast developing technical
product sectors.

Technical Standards for Places of Entertainment *ABTT/DSA* **£30.00** ISBN 1904031056
Technical Standards for Places of Entertainment details the necessary physical standards
required for entertainment venues.

Theatre Engineering and Stage Machinery *Toshiro Ogawa* **£30.00** ISBN 1904031021
Theatre Engineering and Stage Machinery is a unique reference work covering every aspect
of theatrical machinery and stage technology in global terms, and across the complete
historical spectrum.

Theatre Lighting in the Age of Gas *Terence Rees* **£24.95** ISBN 190403117X
Entertainment Technology Press has republished this valuable historic work previously
produced by the Society for Theatre Research in 1978. *Theatre Lighting in the Age of Gas*
investigates the technological and artistic achievements of theatre lighting engineers from
the 1700s to the late Victorian period.

Theatre Space: A Rediscovery Reported *Francis Reid* **£19.95** ISBN 1904031439
In the post-war world of the 1950s and 60s, the format of theatre space became a matter for
a debate that aroused passions of an intensity unknown before or since. The proscenium
arch was clearly identified as the enemy, accused of forming a barrier to disrupt the relations
between the actor and audience. An uneasy fellow-traveller at the time, Francis Reid later
recorded his impressions whilst enjoying performances or working in theatres old and new
and this book is an important collection of his writings in various theatrical journals from
1969-2001 including his contribution to the Cambridge Guide to the Theatre in 1988. It
reports some of the flavour of the period when theatre architecture was rediscovering its past
in a search to establish its future.

Theatres of Achievement *John Higgins* **£29.95** ISBN: 1904031374
John Higgins affectionately describes the history of 40 distinguished UK theatres in a
personal tribute, each uniquely illustrated by the author. Completing each profile is colour
photography by Adrian Eggleston.

Walt Disney Concert Hall – The Backstage Story *Patricia MacKay & Richard Pilbrow*
£28.95 ISBN 1904031234
Spanning the 16-year history of the design and construction of the Walt Disney Concert
Hall, this book provides a fresh and detailed behind the scenes story of the design and
technology from a variety of viewpoints. This is the first book to reveal the "process" of the
design of a concert hall.

Yesterday's Lights – A Revolution Reported *Francis Reid* **£26.95** ISBN 1904031323
Set to help new generations to be aware of where the art and science of theatre lighting is
coming from – and stimulate a nostalgia trip for those who lived through the period, Francis
Reid's latest book has over 350 pages dedicated to the task, covering the 'revolution' from
the fifties through to the present day. Although this is a highly personal account of the
development of lighting design and technology and he admits that there are 'gaps', you'd be
hard put to find anything of significance missing.

Go to www.etbooks.co.uk for full details of above titles and secure online ordering facilities.